The Surelock Commentary on the *Book of James*

A Bible Study from a Different Perspective

Roger Riccard

First published in 2023 by
The Irregular Special Press
for Baker Street Studios Ltd
Endeavour House
170 Woodland Road, Sawston
Cambridge, CB22 3DX, UK

Overall © Baker Street Studios Ltd, 2023
Text © remains with the author, 1998

All rights reserved

No parts of this publication may be reproduced, stored in retrieval systems or transmitted in any form or by any means, electronic, mechanical, photocopying, recording or otherwise, except brief extracts for the purposes of review, without prior permission of the publishers.

Any paperback edition of this book, whether published simultaneously with, or subsequent to, the case bound edition, is sold subject to the condition that it shall not by way of trade, be lent, resold, hired out or otherwise disposed of without the publisher's consent, in any form of binding or cover other than that in which it was published.

Biblical quotes contained herein are from
The Holy Bible New King James Version
Copyright © 1982 by Thomas Nelson, Inc.

ISBN: 1 901091 87 2 (10 digit)
ISBN: 978 1 901091 87 8 (13 digit)

Cover Concept: Roger Riccard
Shell icon courtesy of openclipart.org

Typeset in 8/11/20pt Palatino

About the Author

Roger Riccard, though born and raised in the USA, has Scottish roots, which trace his lineage back to the Rose clan of the Highlands in Scotland. This British Isles ancestry encouraged his interest in the writings of Sir Arthur Conan Doyle and C.S. Lewis. He is now the author of over fifty stories featuring mysteries with the 'World's First Consulting Detective'.

However, once upon a time, he took up biblical studies at Moody Bible Institute in Chicago, IL and earned certifications to teach both *Old* and *New Testament* Adult Bible Studies. In studying what one might term 'the mysteries of religion', he found that the *Book of James* appealed to him most as being a practical guide to living the Christian life. His admiration for C.S. Lewis' work, *The Screwtape Letters*, prompted him to put that concept into use for a biblical study of this *New Testament* letter.

He is also a graduate of California State University, Northridge with Bachelor of Arts degrees in both History and Journalism. He currently resides in a suburb of Los Angeles, CA where he busies himself reading and writing mysteries and singing with a group which entertains senior citizens at retirement homes.

Other Books by Roger Riccard

Sherlock Holmes & The Case of the Poisoned Lilly

Sherlock Holmes & The Case of the Twain Papers

Sherlock Holmes: Adventures for the Twelve Days of Christmas

Sherlock Holmes: Further Adventures for the Twelve Days of Christmas

A Sherlock Holmes Alphabet of Cases Volume One: A-E

A Sherlock Holmes Alphabet of Cases Volume Two: F-J

A Sherlock Holmes Alphabet of Cases Volume Three: K-O

A Sherlock Holmes Alphabet of Cases Volume Four: P-T

A Sherlock Holmes Alphabet of Cases Volume Five: U-Z

The Colourful Cases of Sherlock Holmes Volume One

To my Ultimate Saviour, Jesus the Christ.
And to my Rosilyn, who is now with Him,
but who gave me the best years of my life.

Reviewed by Edith Wairimu for Readers' Favorite

Written in a satirical style similar to *The Screwtape Letters* by C. S. Lewis, *The Surelock Commentary on the Book of James: A Bible Study from a Different Perspective* by Roger Riccard is an eye-opening examination of the teachings found in *James*. It takes an epistolary format in which a senior demon, Surelock, guides his subordinate, Wantsome, on how to subvert the instructions provided in the *Book of James* and keep believers from reading the Book. Surelock suggests techniques that Wantsome can use to discourage and deceive his charges while manipulating them. The work examines each chapter, addressing commonly held misconceptions about specific passages. It shows how the teachings provided are especially relevant in today's world and encourages Christians to remain vigilant and aware of demonic strategies.

The work is a critical reminder to believers of the enemy we face and the tactics the devil uses to tempt Christians and undervalue biblical teachings. I appreciated how the book shows the relevance and importance of the *Book of James* in combatting current issues faced by churches and Christian communities. Its discussions about the misinterpretations of certain verses are thought-provoking and it aptly tackles the theological topics shared in James. While entertaining, Surelock's observations and suggestions are also jarring. The *Surelock Commentary on the Book of James* by Roger Riccard is a timely, compelling work that is bound to stir readers into action and encourage them to avoid complacency. Readers will love the work's style and will find its observations enlightening. Highly recommended.

Author's Note

In 1940 renown Christian author C. S. Lewis conceived the idea of *The Screwtape Letters* in which 'His Abysmal Sublimity Under-Secretary Screwtape' gives advice to his Nephew, Wormwood, an entry-level tempter going out on his first assignment.

These devils have but one aim, to confound the true aspects of Christianity so that their subjects might not ever come to a saving faith in 'that One Whose Name we do not speak; the Son of the Enemy'.

Shortly after completion, the *Letters* were issued in weekly installments by the church news magazine, *The Guardian*, from May through November 1941. They were first published in book form by the firm of Geoffrey Bles Ltd. of London in 1942 and came to America in 1943 under the publishing of the Macmillan Company.

In this tribute, we examine the correspondence between a new Under-Secretary, Surelock, and his demon pupil, Wantsome, who has charge over several subjects rather than just one. These potential victims have entered into a Bible Study of the *Book of James* and Surelock feels compelled to instruct Wantsome via his commentary on the epistle.

It is hoped that this commentary from 'the other side', like Lewis' original work, will be both entertaining and enlightening in helping Christians overcome temptation and pursue righteousness. If it stirs the brethren out of complacency and into action, so much the better. The spiritual warfare taking place in America is in great need of soldiers willing to follow James' admonition to 'prove their faith by their works' or the battle may soon be lost.

There are 'giants in the land', the internet, movies, television, magazines, the news media, political action groups, profiteering corporations, the pornography industry, evolutionists, secular humanists, socialists, communists, anti-Christian educators, and on and on. Many of these giants seem to be controlled by the forces of Satan and appear invincible because of the growth they've enjoyed while 'Christian America' has slept and failed to put its' faith into works.

Like Joshua and Caleb, we must cry out "the Lord is with us, do not fear them!" But one word of caution before you go into battle, you must remember who the enemy is.

> *For we do not wrestle against flesh and blood,*
> *but against principalities, against powers,*
> *against the rulers of darkness of this age,*
> *against spiritual hosts of wickedness in*
> *the heavenly places.*
>
> *Ephesians 6: 12*

Yes, we must fight the battle, but remember that our greatest weapon is love. Love doesn't have to mean passive non-resistance. That would be Surelock's advice. The 'Enemy's Handbook', as he refers to the Bible, tells us that love confronts, love disciplines, and love requires action. The people involved with the evil 'giants' are not the enemy, they are a mission field. They need to be told that Christianity is not dead. If they can be brought to understand that the answers they are seeking are to be found in Christ rather than in the 'cause' they now serve, their uniting under God can bring down the 'giants' and send Surelock and Wantsome scurrying back to 'their Father Below'.

Roger Riccard

Introduction

My Dear Wantsome,

Of all the writings that are contained within the Enemy's Handbook, there is one in particular that I would recommend to you to steer your subjects clear of. Since you have such a poor record at keeping your charges from reading the blessed thing, at least endeavour to distract them from getting into the book written by that wretched apostle James.

It contains passages of the most disgusting practicality for the believer in that One who's Name we do not speak. It is, however, also a book that is easy for us to use to manipulate and discourage when applied properly. I trust that should you come across anyone studying these passages you will apply all the techniques at your command to make them aware of the disadvantages that following James' advice would bring them in the everyday world they must live and work in.

For those occasions, I will be sending along some further comments regarding this infamous book that will help you in your temptations of the disgusting little creatures that the Enemy has chosen to be His children.

The Surelock Commentary on the *Book of James*

In the meantime, I trust you will be diligent in your duties and follow the admonition of Our Father Below expressed in his prime directive, "To hell with everybody!"

Under Secretary of Eternal State
Surelock

Memo One

James 1:1

First of all, my young colleague, you might let it become known to your subjects that there has been much controversy over the *Book of James* throughout the centuries. There still exists doubt among humans as to who the original author really was. The Son of the carpenter had two disciples by that name. One being the brother of John (another prolific writer!) and the other being the son of Alphaeus. A third James is mentioned in the crucifixion accounts as James the less, a son of Mary. It has not been established, however, which Mary is referred to. Thus, there is no way to be sure if this is the same James as the brother of the One crucified. That leaves four potential candidates for authorship. Though most of them agree upon James, His brother, there are arguments in favour of the others. This fact alone can be your doorway to doubts in the minds of your subjects. By implanting the proper thoughts, you can hang them up on this question alone for enough time as may delay their entry into a serious study of the book itself. This is most useful in a group study situation where you can create an air of boredom and discourage some people from ever coming back to hear future topics.

What you must not let them realize is that the authorship of the book is not nearly as important as the lessons contained within. If they start remembering that all scripture is inspired by the Enemy they will become satisfied with that fact alone.

There are other tactics of this type that you might bring to bear. Point out to your subjects all the shortcomings of the book that might render it unworthy of serious consideration. Since it is generally believed to have been written by Mary's second son then its authorship was not by a disciple. Nor was it written by that accursed Paul who is responsible for most of the *New Testament* in the Enemy's Handbook. Lacking such credentials as these how important could it be?

The Surelock Commentary on the *Book of James*

The book is only five chapters in length. Could something that small really be significant? One of my personal favorites is the argument that Martin Luther, looked up to as a founder of Protestant Christianity, could not bring himself to include the *Book of James* in his canon. It gives me glee to think how that man, despite all the trouble he caused us, could have made the mistake of misinterpreting James' emphasis on works as contradictory to Paul's admonition that men are saved by faith alone. It will be most useful for us to twist that thinking toward our ends for these latter generations.

But to continue with your strategy lesson, the opening statement of the book is thus:

> **1** James, a bondservant and of the Lord Jesus Christ, to the twelve tribes which are scattered abroad, greetings.

The address to the twelve tribes can also be useful in your distraction of the reader. The immediate thought is that this letter is for the Jews scattered throughout the Roman Empire. It would be well to encourage that thinking so that your subjects will be tempted to reject this writing as being only for those with a Jewish background. If you can keep the wretches from finding that James was writing to his Christian brothers, perhaps they won't pursue it any further.

It is also important that they not realize the significance of James referring to himself as a bond-servant. It is, in fact, an identification of the true leadership that the Carpenter spoke of when He says that he who would be the greatest must be the servant of all.

Altogether Wantsome, your primary goal is to stop your subjects from reading this book. Its practicality is too objectionable to our way of thinking. The human who takes James' letter to heart can cause us much trouble. Remember the words of Our Father Below:

'Study of the Enemy's Handbook is something we must interfere. Keep your subjects distracted and someday they'll join us here.'

STUDY QUESTIONS FOR MEMO ONE

What are some of the ways that Satan may use to distract us from a study of the book of James?

Matthew 20:26 quotes Jesus discussing true servanthood. Read the passage from verse 20-28 and then list your own definition of a servant.

James was one of the first *New Testament* books to be written. Its five chapters contain fifty-four commands in one hundred and eight verses. Why do you suppose James was writing with such authoritative style at this point in church history?

The 'twelve tribes dispersed abroad' refers to more than just the Jewish Nation. Why do you think James would use this salutation when writing to fellow Christians?

What is a bond-servant?

In what ways can you exhibit the fact that you are also a bond-servant of Jesus Christ?

Memo Two
James 1:2-4

So, Wantsome, you haven't been able to completely discourage your subjects from a study of the *Book of James*. Very well, if they insist on continuing you must redouble your efforts in distracting them and leading their study off on to unimportant tangents. In doing so you may cause them to miss out on the jewels of knowledge contained within.

Let us look at the next few verses of that first chapter.

> 2 *My brethren, count it all joy when you fall into various trials,*
> 3 *knowing that the testing of your faith produces patience.*
> 4 *But let patience have its perfect work, that you may be perfect and complete, lacking nothing.*

Now, of course, it is obvious that you must point out to them what utter nonsense verse two attempts to encourage. Who in their right mind is going to enjoy the trials of life? James appears to be some sort of masochist to make a statement like that. Just be sure to keep the vermin from reading their footnotes or commentaries and discovering that the Greek word for 'all' also means 'pure'. We don't want them to realize that James is advocating a purity of joy in their hearts that allows them a close communion with the Enemy. He is telling them not to fake joyfulness out of some religious obligation, but to be truly joyful because of the knowledge they have that the Son of the carpenter will help them endure. But WHY must their faith be tested? This is the question you must stir within them. Fan the sparks of doubt into flames of disenchantment before they realize that it is not for the purpose of punishment that the Enemy tests. Nor is it even He doing the testing when there is a temptation to sin involved.

An important factor for you to keep in mind is that their thoughts may automatically take them to the *Book of Job*. You must do everything in your power to stop them from developing a second study of that portion of the Enemy's handbook. Digression and tangents are fine but they should lead away from a study of the Enemy's ways and means, not toward a deeper understanding of them. In this case, a study of Job would reveal too much of our strategy and if all humankind were to learn to react as Job did, they would be improved by their capacity for endurance. As James puts it, they will become more and more perfect as these attitudes take effect in their lives. The man who endures by faith will find his faith growing and enabling him to become more than ever like the Son. If your subjects learn to practice this type of faith, they will someday find themselves approaching a completeness in which they will lack nothing. Indeed, they will be assured of an ultimate crown of life totally beyond the cares of the world in which they are now confined.

For Beelzebub's sake don't let them find *Romans 8:28* where Paul tells them "And we know all things work together for good to those who love God and are called according to His purpose."

This is dangerous thinking for them to become involved in Wantsome. You must concentrate their minds on the worries and cares of their everyday existence. If you fail to sow the seeds of doubt, your only alternative is to lead them to the extreme of becoming so heavenly-minded that they are no earthly good. While this tactic has its purpose, they are far more useful to us as doubters and scoffers.

Mind yourself Wantsome, Your subjects are treading dangerous ground. Whereas James sees trials as an opportunity for growth toward perfection you must encourage the little dust-balls to see trials as circumstances

Memo Two

that they must get through and then go on. Don't ever let them discover trials to be learning experiences. As long as these times are nothing but bad memories, we have an excellent foothold for temptation. And temptation, Wantsome, is our business. Remember your training:

> Tempt them! Tempt them ! But never let it show. Tempt them always, wherever they may go. Be subtle, be sneaky, be harsh and be cruel, make each one feel like nothing but a fool!
>
> Tempters Chant No. 6

STUDY QUESTIONS FOR MEMO TWO

How would you respond to someone who tells you that good can come from the trials which you are experiencing?

What good has ever come out of a situation where you experienced trials?

What attitude did James tell people to exhibit when facing trials?

What is produced when our faith is tested?

What reward awaits a person who perseveres under trial?

What does it mean to be 'perfect and complete'?

How does the story of Job help you when facing trials?

Memo Three
James 1:5-8

Now, Wantsome, we are about to get into it. The next few passages in that dreadful letter really can open up opportunities for you. As you recall it reads thus:

> 5 *If any of you lacks wisdom, let him ask of God, who gives to all liberally and without reproach, and it will be given to him.*
> 6 *But let him ask in faith, with no doubting, for he who doubts is like a wave of the sea driven and tossed by the wind.*
> 7 *For let not that man suppose that he will receive anything from the Lord;*
> 8 *he is a doubleminded man, unstable in all his ways.*

It is essential that you instill a sense of pride in your subjects at this point, Wantsome. Do not let them recognize their own need for the Enemy's wisdom. No one wants to admit to being foolish or stupid. Play on that thought and keep them away from reading *I Corinthians* 1:25 and Paul's comments regarding the wisdom of God as compared to men. By keeping them from recognizing their need they will not ask to have it filled.

Should they summon the intelligence in their tiny little brains to actually ask for wisdom, then it is up to you to sow the seeds of doubt. The scripture says that He gives generously and without reproach, but come now! Is this really true? The Enemy is actually going to give away wisdom to just anybody without reservation? Of course, that's where the acceptance and faith without doubt come in, but don't let your subjects think of that.

The Surelock Commentary on the *Book of James*

Doubt is our greatest weapon, Wantsome. Ever since Our Father below first encountered Eve in the Garden we have found it to be a key ingredient in our recipe for human suffering. I would refer you to page four of your Tempter's Manual where you will find a complete list of possibilities, but for a quick rundown here are some approaches you might consider:

- I don't need God.
- God just wants me for a slave.
- God doesn't care.
- God always says 'no'.
- God wants me to do things I don't want to do.
- I never get any revelations or clear-cut answers from God.
- God's too busy for my trivial problems.
- God takes too long.
- This other way is easier.
- I know what's best for me. Why doesn't God do it?

Of course, these ten temptations are mere coal in the bonfire, but you get the idea. The Enemy has endowed these creatures with just enough intelligence to question and test everything when they think of it, and even one of them was clever enough to realize that a little knowledge is a dangerous thing. Beelzebub realized that long ago when he coerced Eve into eating the fruit from the tree of knowledge. Since then, we have enjoyed the company of many of her offspring because of their self-proclaimed wisdom. Keep instilling your subjects with pride and we'll enjoy the company of many more.

The Enemy unfortunately gave James a fair portion of wisdom when he wrote this passage. He gives strict warnings against doubting and being double-minded. It was as though he knew these would be the weapons we would use. At this point, you must keep your subjects from referring to the *Gospel of Matthew*. That turncoat tax-collector recorded the promises of that One Whose Name we do not speak in chapter 7 verses 7-11. 'Ask and it will be given unto you', indeed! I cannot

Memo Three

emphasize enough how important it is for you to distract your charges from this step of faith. Unfortunately, this step is one of the basics of belief. In *Proverbs* 3:5-8 they are told:

> *5 Trust in the Lord with all your heart, and do not lean on your own understanding*
> *6 In all your ways acknowledge Him, and He will make your paths straight*
> *7 Do not be wise in your own eyes; Fear the Lord and turn away from evil.*
> *8 It will be a healing to your body and refreshment to your bones.*

Such basic simple-minded faith makes me gag! Throw yourself into your work, Wantsome, and tempt your victims to seek out all the available methods of solving their problems. Make them not only double-minded but triple- and quadruple-minded! Fill their thoughts with so many variations and doubts that they will indeed be tossed to and fro like the waves of the sea. This concept of trusting in Him for wisdom is too basic a foundation for you to let the despicable piles of protoplasm stand on. Doubt, Wantsome, that's your weapon. Doubt! Doubt! Doubt!

> A-doubting they will go
> A-doubting they will go
> Until they hit
> the fiery pit
> A-doubting they will go
>
> Tempter's Hymnal

The Surelock Commentary on the *Book of James*

STUDY QUESTIONS FOR MEMO THREE

What doubts do you have about God responding to your prayers?

Can doubting affect your prayer life? How?

When have you ever received wisdom from God? How did you receive it?

What type of 'wisdom' do you suppose James is referring to? What other types are there?

Look again at the 10 excuses Surelock lists as doubts that cause us not to pray. Do any of them sound familiar to you? What will you do to avoid falling into that trap again in the future?

One good way to get over negative doubts is to look for positive aspects. Make a list of the positive things God does in your life that you usually take for granted. This can be your first step in learning how much you really can trust God for what's best in your life.

Memo Four

James 1:9-11

At this time, Wantsome, we must discuss something very near and dear to the hearts of all mankind. Something that has inspired murder and mayhem, wars and riots, and an endless list of sins.

MONEY

Some people you can talk to until you're blue in the face (pardon the expression) and it won't affect them one iota. But hit them in their wallet and you have their utmost attention. Unfortunately, James has chosen to address this topic in his writings in an effort to weaken our stranglehold. Again in chapter one he writes:

> **9** *Let the lowly brother glory in his exaltation,*
> **10** *but the rich in his humiliation, because as a flower of the field he will pass away.*
> **11** *For no sooner has the sun risen with a burning heat than it withers the grass; its flower falls, and its beautiful appearance perishes. So the rich man also will fade away in his pursuits.*

James is attempting to get his readers to glory or be happy in their humble circumstances because there are riches awaiting them in the Enemy's Kingdom. This is the 'high position' he refers to. But don't let your readers realize that. James' wording is unusual in translation and on the surface sounds like he is advocating poverty and rebuking wealth. Encourage this thinking, Wantsome. Let your subjects think that Christianity denounces material possessions as evil and sinful. That will certainly cool their enthusiasm.

That One Whose Name we do not speak also taught of the folly of riches in a number of his parables. The rich young ruler and the rich fool who tore down his barns come to mind. He even said that it was easier for a camel to go through the eye of a needle than for a rich man to enter the Enemy's Kingdom.

This should disillusion your subjects. It can appear highly confusing for them to look upon riches as a result of the Enemy's blessing when the Enemy tells them that riches are a humiliation.

What James is doing is echoing Paul's statement in his first letter to the Corinthians. In verse 31 of chapter 7 (How clever of the little ragamuffins to devise Scripture addresses!) he tells the brethren from now on 'those who use the world (should be) as those who did not make full use of it; for the form of this world is passing away'.

You must not allow them to dwell on these things, Wantsome. If they should start looking at material things as meaningless you will lose tremendous advantages over them. If they start quoting that old cliché about being 'in the world but not of the world', flaunt all the nice worldly possessions of their neighbours in front of them. Bigger homes in nicer areas, expensive cars with fancy options, the newest fashions in clothing, all of the latest audio-visual-computer equipment for home entertainment, and the best of whatever is the latest fad. These are the sort of things with which to tempt them. Naturally, you must also provide them with some lofty excuse to satisfy their conscience, but any fool can justify his folly, especially with our help.

In *Philippians* 4:11-12 Paul speaks of contentment in all circumstances:

> "Not that I speak in regard to need, for I have learned in whatever state I am, to be content: I know how to be abased and I know how to abound Everywhere and in all things I have learned both to be full and to be hungry, both to abound and to suffer need "

Memo Four

That One Whose Name we do not speak has an irritating habit of supplying the needs of all who trust Him. And striving for more and more is vanity, as King Solomon discovered so many centuries ago. It is merely an exercise in futility in trying to satisfy wants that can never be satisfied by earthly goods.

Fortunately for us, many have reversed Solomon's example by going after material goods instead of first asking for the Enemy's wisdom and then having their riches bestowed upon them.

Our Father Below is also the Father of Lies and one of his best is that wealth brings happiness. Most of your subjects are smart enough to realize that mere possessions have no lasting value but they seem to think that having those possessions can improve their relationships with other people and that these relationships will lead to happiness. This, however, is not the truth but a clever scheme on Our Father's part. Relationships based upon the admiration of material goods are shallow indeed. There is no desire to help each other, only to be equal to or better than one another.

What the creatures fail to realize is that the best of everything on this earthly sphere is but a pale shadow of what awaits them in the Enemy's Kingdom. Even more, the brief span of life they spend on this planet is but a speck of their eternal existence. But all that is to our advantage, Wantsome. As you will recall from your Time and Material Concepts class at Tempters College:

> "The human-kind have no true concept of eternity. This fact, coupled with their great propensity for impatience, is of great benefit to you in your work as tempters. They want everything 'now' and because of their love for material goods, you can use many types of temptations to sin so that they might achieve their desire. For so many of them, the end does indeed justify the means. Little do they realize that material ends are worthless in eternity.

They seem to feel their reward in 'Glory' will be based on their accumulations during their brief appearance on this current world. Use that erroneous thinking to your advantage demons, and you will deliver their souls to Beelzebub on a silver platter. "

Professor Goldclock

Memo Four

STUDY QUESTIONS FOR MEMO FOUR

What's wrong with money?

What eventually happens to the wealth of a rich man?

Have you ever been disappointed in your pursuit of wealth?

How have material possessions disappointed you once you've gained them?

What are some ways you could learn to be content in your circumstances?

What are some of the dangers of pursuing humility? How will you avoid them?

Memo Five

James 1:12-15

I must now speak to you regarding temptation, Wantsome. The next section of James' letter deals with overcoming temptation and unfortunately reveals some basic tenets of our strategies for capturing people's souls. It reads thus:

> **12** *Blessed is a man who endures under temptation; for when he has been approved, he will receive the crown of life which the Lord has promised to those who love Him.*
> **13** *Let no one say when he is tempted, "I am tempted by God"; for God cannot be tempted by evil, nor does He Himself tempt anyone.*
> **14** *But each one is tempted when he is drawn away by his own desires and enticed.*
> **15** *Then, when desire has conceived, it gives birth to sin; and sin, when it is full-grown, brings forth death.*

This passage is full of possibilities for you my fiendish friend. First of all, you may implant the question *'Why* must I be tempted?'. This can lead to many doubts about the sovereignty of the Enemy and a questioning of His wisdom and fairness. The opening statement appears to require that the 'crown of life' must be earned by persevering trial i.e. resisting temptation. If this be the case whatever happened to the free gift of salvation? Was Martin Luther correct? Is James preaching a different doctrine than Paul? Unfortunately for us, this is not so. The approval spoken of is faith in the Carpenter. When this faith is used to overcome temptations, it shows that it is real faith proven by works and not empty rhetoric.

The next verse states that the Enemy cannot be tempted by evil. Bring back to the minds of your subjects some of the *Old Testament* stories about the destruction of cities, nations, and even the world by the Almighty Himself. Was not the killing of so many creatures evil? We, of course, know better. The Enemy only destroyed the evil, that which we had firmly infiltrated. But it is often useful for us to point to the 'angry' Being of the *Old Testament* as we plant doubts in our victims' minds.

Even in the *New Testament* the Son of Mary is reported as being tempted for forty days. Doesn't this contradict James' statement that He cannot be tempted? Or does it reveal that the Carpenter is not, in fact, equal to His Father?

What you must not let your subject realize is that within the Son there was also complete humanity. The human mind allows us many avenues of access. Unfortunately, His was so disciplined and filled with faith that He was able to resist everything with which Our Father Below enticed Him. His calling Himself the 'Son of Man' has confused the piddly brains of many human scholars. But this ability to resist temptation is just one aspect of a new personality that all the vermin will someday achieve if we fail to capture them first. The 'Son of Man' is just that, the next step in human evolution, a result of accepting the Enemy and His Son and receiving a new body in the coming kingdom. The Enemy's Handbook tells them they will all be changed and when the Carpenter walked on the planet, they had the opportunity to see their future selves. We are fortunate indeed that so few of them understand this. If they did, then James' next verse would be meaningless because they would never give in to their lusts.

James has done us a favour at this point, however. He tells his readers that they are responsible for their own temptations. There is no mention of us or Lucifer and the part we often play in those temptations.

Of course, they *are* ultimately responsible. The desires and lusts in their hearts are the results of their own doing. We merely build on those foundations within each individual's personality. We know what their weaknesses are. All we need

Memo Five

to do is distract their thinking from spiritual desires to physical desires. Once distracted, they easily fall.

A prime example of this is Peter the fisherman. When he saw the Carpenter walking on the water, he was bold enough to step out on faith. So long as he kept his eyes on Him, he was fine, but once he began looking around at the physical peril surrounding him, he panicked and sank. His fears caused him to lose sight of his Savior and long for the security of the boat. He, like most of the clumsy clumps of clay, failed to realize that all things are possible through the Son so long as they fix their minds on Him rather than the world. The things awaiting them are so much better than what the world offers it gives me great pleasure to turn them away with a well-planned enticement. It just burns me to think that the Enemy is willing to give the disgusting creatures even more than we had when we chose to follow Our Father Below.

But on to the final verse. James has outlined our battle plan precisely in his observation. We fan the spark in their mind and if done correctly it will burst into flame at just the opportune moment. Too much and it is blown out by the gale force and the recognition, by the victim, of its ultimate harm. Too little and it dies from lack of fuel. But if you do your job correctly, Wantsome, you will set their souls afire and bring them into Hell's inferno.

Always remember, however, while James is correct in his conclusion that sin brings forth death, there is always the option of repentance and crying out to the One Whose Name we do not speak. He has a tender and merciful heart toward the creatures and commands the power to cast us aside. Take great care or you'll find yourself at His mercy.

Should a case like this occur, however, you still have some hope. Like a house swept clean, if your subject fails to maintain his diligence and takes his situation for granted it is extremely easy to catch him off guard and lure him into sin all over again, so never give up!

Amazing lust
how sweet the power
that fills their hearts with sin

They could be saved
but now they're ours
they're blind to what they're in

                    Tempter's Hymnal

Memo Five

STUDY QUESTIONS FOR MEMO FIVE

Why are we subjected to trials?

Where does temptation come from?

If we know where temptation comes from, why do we so often give in to it?

What is the true relationship between our actions and our salvation?

How do we overcome enticements to sin?

Memo Six

James 1:16-18

The subject of this memo, my dear, Wantsome, is the consistency of the Enemy. A problem that plagues us but also allows us access to the questioning minds of the human pests. James addresses it thus:

> **16** *Do not be deceived, my beloved brethren.*
> **17** *Every good gift and every perfect gift is from above, and comes down from the Father of lights, with whom there is no variation or shadow of turning.*
> **18** *Of his own will He brought us forth by the word of truth, that we might be a kind of firstfruits of His creatures.*

Sin, of course, is always deceptive. The fools would never sin if they didn't think the results of their actions would be more rewarding than a sinless life. Deception has been our weapon from the beginning. In the Garden, Eve stated that she was deceived by the serpent and she was so right. Of course, it was her new-found knowledge that enabled her to identify deception and her descendants have been a most suspicious lot ever since then. But don't let that stop you, Wantsome. Getting them to believe a lie will soon lead them into living a lie. You know the routine, put some truth in every lie to tickle itching ears. Once they've been deceived it becomes quite easy to build upon their desires with temptation. After they've succumbed to their lust it gets even easier to goad them into repeat performances and to embolden them to try new sins. Should his readers heed James' warning about our prime weapon, however, you must do everything you can to impress upon the vermin that they are not, in fact, receiving the gifts promised in verse 17.

The Surelock Commentary on the *Book of James*

Naturally, we do not bestow perfect gifts upon our quivering quarry. Only the Enemy can do that. What you must do then, is to deceive them into thinking that what they gain by following our path is better for them. Fortunately, when they think of a gift it is usually in the material sense and it's always easy to convince them that they're not getting everything they deserve. You must not let them think about that term 'good and perfect' too long, however. Should they realize that nothing in the material world is good and perfect, they will conclude that James is referring to spiritual gifts.

It is interesting that James refers to the Enemy as the 'Father of Lights'. When Our Father Below served in heaven he was known as Lucifer, the angel of light. It is this characteristic that allows him to be so successful at deception. With Satan, however, the imitation of the Enemy is incomplete due to the shifting shadows of the Prince of Darkness.

That despicably practical book of *Proverbs* calls the Enemy a dependable friend who 'sticks closer than a brother' (*Proverbs* 18:24). Paul's first letter to the Thessalonians states that the Enemy is the 'One to be trusted and what He promises, He will do.' (*1 Thessalonians* 5:24). This consistency is always true but not always on the same timetable that the restless rabble would prefer, so you must use this to your advantage. The Enemy's Handbook says that 'Patience is a gift' but don't let it be one of those which your subjects ask for. An impatient human is much easier prey for us.

The next phrase in James' passage is literally translated 'begat' or 'produced'. Thus, when James says that the Enemy brought them forth, he is referring to their new birth in the Carpenter. The phrase 'born again' is the most common term, referring to the Son of Man's discussion with Nicodemus in *John* 3:3. It has been most fortunate for our cause that we have been able to dilute the power and meaning of that term in much the same way that the term 'Christian' no longer holds the meaning it once did. By attracting humans from all spectrums to label themselves 'born again' we have actually discouraged people away from the church. When all sorts of 'weirdoes',

Memo Six

'crazies' and 'undesirables' jump on the bandwagon it helps us all the more.

Of course, it doesn't even have to be the extreme sort that turns people off. The neighbourhood gossip or the fellow who tells the dirty jokes at work can be just as effective as a negative witness for the Enemy's Kingdom.

But I digress. The point is, as His children, born anew in Spirit, James claims that they are the first fruits of the Enemy's creatures. Under Jewish Levitical law, the first fruits of any crop belonged to God. He desired the best of everything up to the first tenth. James' readers, being Jewish followers of the Messiah, were familiar with this law and understood that as the first believers they would be sown into the world to raise up newer and better crops. They could only do this by faith and trust which James emphasizes can be theirs due to the Enemy's consistency and generosity.

That is why all but one of the Nazarene's closest companions died a martyr's death. They knew the truth. They had seen the resurrected Messiah and death no longer held them in fear. As first fruits, they knew the seeds planted by their deaths would flourish and yield those crops that will make the Enemy's final harvest so plentiful. But we'll get our share, Wantsome! Just remain diligent to the task before you.

It might be useful to point out the parable where the seed is sown and so much is wasted. (*Matthew* 13) It could be most discouraging to them if you were to emphasize the barren ground, the rocky soil, and all the other negative aspects of their witness. If you manipulate them properly you can leave them in great despair over the fact that they never seem to find that 'good soil' that yields hundred-fold crops.

I leave you with the words of our dread lord Lucifer:

> "While the Enemy's agents are sowing seeds of good works it is up to you, my young demons to be sowing the seeds of temptation. The sins we trap them into are like weeds. The seeds find the tiniest of cracks in their spirits and implant

themselves firmly. When neglected and left to grow too long they will become extremely difficult to remove for the roots are firmly entrenched.

There are also the weeds that find dark hidden corners and flourish unknown until that area is needed and then it is found to be choked off. But if you allow the seed to be detected when it first sends out its shoots it can be all too easily uprooted for it has not had the time to stretch deep into their lives. Be subtle my young fiends. Subtlety is the key."

Address to the Freshman Class,
Tempter's College

STUDY QUESTIONS FOR MEMO SIX

Where do good and perfect gifts come from?

Besides your salvation, what is the best gift you've ever received?

How do you feel about the person who gave it to you?

What should be our response to God concerning the gifts He's given us?

Why are we sometimes fooled into sin?

How can we avoid sin's 'shifting shadows'?

What is our responsibility as God's 'first fruits'?

Memo Seven

James 1:19-21

Now, Wantsome, we move on to the interesting subject of communication. James, at this point, turns his address to the art of effective communication and you must be ready to combat it at all costs. His comments read as follows:

> **19** *So then, my beloved brethren, let every man be swift to hear, slow to speak, slow to wrath;*
> **20** *for the wrath of man does not produce the righteousness of God*
> **21** *Therefore lay aside all filthiness and overflow of wickedness, and receive with meekness the implanted word, which is able to save your souls.*

Many of humankind have been exposed to the exhortation 'When you see the word 'Therefore' look and see what it's there for. It's usually followed by a command'. Of course, such is the case in this piece of scribble from James. Unfortunately, there is the wisdom of the Enemy behind James' words so you must be very resourceful as you strike your subjects with the slings of confusion and the arrows of lies.

Let us rip apart James' comments one by one. First of all, no one can control the speed at which he hears. In fact, the speed of sound is quite constant and the noise one hears is variable only by the object producing it. What you must not let your victim realize is that the true meaning is really not 'be swift' but rather to take the time first to listen and understand what is really being communicated. The idea is to make listening a priority. As one of the clever little vermin put it

'We were given two ears and one mouth so we could listen twice as much as we talk'.

But even more importantly, Wantsome, is that you must not let them realize that being 'swift to hear' applies to their listening to communication from the Enemy even more than to each other. Fortunately, most of them are so busy with the hassles of life we give them, that they fail to realize that He is there at all times, just waiting for them to call on Him so He can give them guidance and answers. This is especially important for you, should you allow them to actually get into a prayer mode. You must keep them talking and talking and talking. This makes it so easy for you to point out that the Enemy doesn't hear their prayers when really, they just aren't taking the time to listen for His answers.

That brings us to James' next comment. When one of them thinks he should be slow to speak remind him of that old human adage 'He who hesitates is lost'.

Fortunately, most of them are better versed in these human sayings than in the Enemy's Handbook. If your subject were to read Solomon's book, he might find this statement instead: 'He who has knowledge spares his words and a man of understanding is of a quiet spirit. Even a fool is counted wise when he holds his peace. When he shuts his lips, he is considered perceptive'. (*Proverbs* 17:27-28) (Note: The famous American President, Abraham Lincoln, paraphrased this verse 'Better to remain silent and be thought a fool, than to speak out and remove all doubt'. It never fails to amaze me how the little pea brains can come up with such pearls of wisdom!)

What James is really trying to get across is merely reemphasizing his first point. By being slow to speak they will naturally become swift to hear. They will have a chance to form an intelligent opinion before opening their disproportionately big mouths and therefore avoid many arguments, hard feelings and misunderstandings. In their communication with the Enemy, they may even find themselves struck dumb (pun intended) by the awesome power and wisdom of His will for their lives if they just stay quiet long enough to hear it.

The next comment, 'slow to wrath', is indeed a wise

admonition on James' part. He obviously had much experience seeing how tempers flare when people are too quick to speak and don't take the time to listen to what's really being said. By being slow to wrath they gain the time they need to have a chance to really understand each other and communicate. Communication opens the road to understanding and thus allows the love bond between believers to remain firm. Miscommunication, caused by being too quick to wrath, does not produce righteousness but bitterness, jealousy and pride. That's where you hit them, Wantsome! Don't give them time to think, make them react quickly and their failure is our success.

As to filthiness and wickedness, James merely states the obvious. If you can keep their minds bombarded with filth and wickedness that is what will overflow from their lives. But don't make the attack too obvious, Wantsome. Just prick their minds with little things that don't seem to be too serious. Things like the good action/adventure movie with 'just a little too much swearing' or 'only one sex scene and you really didn't see all that much'. Or it could be the joke they repeat that's just a little on the dirty side or the television show they watch just for a break from the routine, a little harmless fantasizing. It's the little things we use that will wear them down dear fellow. After a time, our temptations will be so entrenched in their minds they won't even realize how far they've strayed. Let them think they're walking the straight and narrow until our little detours grow wider and longer and eventually lead them completely off the path.

If you allow them to let the Word become implanted it will indeed save their souls and lose them from our Father's kingdom below. The implanted Word will grow and produce the fruits of the Spirit: Love, joy, peace, patience, kindness, goodness, faithfulness, gentleness and self-control (*Galatians 5:22-23*). If this is what they are full of then this is what will overflow instead of filth and wickedness. You must attack those fruits like tiny insects that bore their way in and weave their path of destruction as they corrupt from within.

Remember your basic training:

'The subjects you encounter are not actually stupid, fellow fiends, merely ignorant of the true nature of the universe. When you 'shackle them with a heavy burden, 'neath a load of guilt and shame' they will recognize their pitiful condition and seek a saviour.

No, it is the subtle infiltration of seemingly harmless activities that will actually mould them toward our purposes. Help them avoid the fruits of the Enemy's Spirit by filling them full of the fat meat of temptation, the sins of the flesh, the lust of the eye and the pride of life. When they've gorged themselves on hors d'oeuvres of sin there will be little room for fruits of spirit.'

Professor Fleafeather

STUDY QUESTIONS FOR MEMO SEVEN

What does it mean to be 'swift to hear'?

Why is being 'slow to speak' important?

Can one be too slow to speak?

How do we practice being 'slow to wrath'?

What is the danger of our wrath arising too quickly?

How do we 'lay aside filthiness and overflow of wickedness'?

Can you think of instances where behaviour that was the 'exception' has now become considered as 'normal' or 'acceptable' in our society?

Are you receiving the 'implanted word' and what affect is it having on your life?

Memo Eight

James 1:22-25

Wantsome you have always been such a disappointment to me in the area that James next contemplates. So often you have failed that this memo will sound like a broken record. But it must be said again, for your subjects are about to read a command from James that, if followed, will multiply the difficulty of your task incomprehensibly. It reads thus:

> 22 But be doers of the word, and not hearers only, deceiving yourselves.
> 23 For if anyone is a hearer of the word and not a doer, he is like a man observing his natural face in a mirror;
> 24 for he observes himself, goes away, and immediately forgets what kind of man he was.
> 25 But he who looks into the perfect law of liberty and continues in it, and is not a forgetful hearer but a doer of the work, this one will be blessed in what he does.

'Doing' the Word of the Enemy is the very heart of James' theology and teaching. He will expound upon this subject to even greater depth later on, but for now we must take this in its context.

As his poignant pen has just proposed, the dullards are to be swift to hear. If you can concentrate their attention on hearing and waiting until they are certain, then they may miss many opportunities to actually 'do'. The key here, is to encourage them to look for detailed, specific circumstances that they feel must be weighed out in their minds.

Fortunately for us, most of them consider service for the Enemy to be attending church services, Enemy Handbook studies, or any of the other myriad of activities they indulge in to satisfy their conscience. They gladly sit and hear and allow their minds to be filled, but fail to put what they hear into practice. James has pinpointed another of our best tactics and you must distract your subjects from it. Religious 'fatheads' are acceptable as long as their religion stays in their heads and fails to reach their feet.

However, in verse 25 James explains how to become a 'doer'. He points to the 'perfect law' which that One Whose Name we do not speak referred to in *Mark* 12:29-31, specifically the second commandment which says 'You shall love your neighbour as yourself'. You, Wantsome, must not let them realize that this is the only grid they need to run situations through before they take action. If they were to ask themselves 'would this be loving to my neighbour?' instead of waiting for some sort of 'sign' from the Enemy I cannot imagine the damage that would be done to our cause.

Some have referred to the observations in the mirror as church attendance. So many of them think that one hour they give each week is enough observance to satisfy the Enemy. This fits our cause but it would be so much better to get them out from under the influence of other believers altogether. If you cannot stop them completely, perhaps you can at least turn them into just occasional 'observers in a mirror' who are easily distracted and can be lured away from the mirror for longer and longer periods of time so that they forget what it is that they are supposed to reflect each and every day.

Another tactic might be to confuse them on the point of 'perfect law of liberty'. What is that exactly? At one point in time, we had convinced some of them that it meant they could do anything, for even sin pointed out how much more perfect the Enemy was and would bring greater blessings the more they had to ask for forgiveness. Unfortunately, that scoundrel Paul put a stop to that in his letter to the Romans. But it might be worth a try, Wantsome, the bumbling little beings do tend to be forgetful.

Memo Eight

James has encouraged them to a course of action which educators of modern times have just recently discovered. That is, since men forget 90% of what they hear but remember 90% of what they do, putting faith into action helps them remember the Enemy's Word and builds up their faith as well as helping out those in need. This 'learning by doing' is most destructive to our cause, Wantsome. You must use any means at your disposal to stop them. The old standbys of fear and shyness work well in these situations. If they do manage to muster their courage then you must twist their efforts askew. Mislead them into doing too much, or in an overzealous manner that offends others. This will cause them to doubt the Enemy's word regarding the 'blessings' promised in verse 25. Don't allow the thought to cross their minds that to be blessed may have nothing to do with their *results,* but in fact, may be a reward for their *efforts* and may come in a completely unrelated way. Manipulate the results they perceive into discouragement and don't forget to tangle them up on theological differences. I can't tell you the joy you will experience when witnessing a good theological debate, even when it is just one of the little mushbrains debating in their own mind.

> Fill their heads, fiends. Oh fill them up fiends.
> Let them strive for knowledge more and more.
> They can read, and read forever, if they choose.
> Just don't let, their faith get out the door.
>
> Tempter's Hymnal

STUDY QUESTIONS FOR MEMO EIGHT

What deception does James refer to when he says 'be doers and not hearers only'?

James has also told us to be swift to hear and slow to speak. How does this relate to our 'doings'?

Surelock points out a real danger here. Can you think of instances where you have been so intent on hearing the word and waiting for just the right sign that you have failed to act when action was needed?

How do you think that looking at our natural face in a mirror relates to our going to church?

How does putting our faith into action help us?

Memo Nine

James 1:26-27

Authentic religion is the next subject of James' address. As a Tempter 2nd class you are well aware of the difference between religion and relationship with the Carpenter. James has continued his 'doers of the word' theme with the following drivel:

> 26 *If anyone among you thinks he is religious, and does not bridle his tongue but deceives his own heart, this one's religion is useless.*
> 27 *Pure and undefiled religion before God and the Father is this: to visit orphans and widows in their trouble, and to keep oneself unspotted from the world.*

We have been fairly successful Wantsome, at convincing many of the mindless morons that ritual, liturgy, and ceremony are the true measure of religion. So long as they practice these they shall be considered 'righteous', and of course, they believe that righteousness will gain them entrance to the Enemy's camp. You must encourage this thinking, Wantsome. Steer them clear of that passage in *Matthew* 7:21-23 where the Son of Man warns against the dangers of following religious practice without knowing the author of the religion. It is so easy for them to be 'deceived in their own hearts' that you should have no trouble at all. They do so wish to avoid facing their own shortcomings so instead, they brag about their religious service, which points out the necessity for James' warning.

Authentic religion is indeed much more than lip service and ritual. James is so practical in his teaching that we have lost many a fine prospect from those who have indulged themselves in the study of his work. Perhaps, in your case, you should concentrate your victim's attention on verse 27 and the admonition to 'visit orphans and widows in their trouble'.

Such visitation alone is next to worthless but James hasn't gone into much detail here. While he is saying religion should be marked by personal ministries, such as involvement in responding to the authentic needs of people, you can turn the literal words to our advantage. If all they do is *visit* these two specific classes of people and then do nothing practical to help them, they will have fulfilled the letter of the law as written here. What you must distract them from is other writings in the Enemy's Handbook that go into much more depth such as *1 John* 3:17 or *Matthew* 15:4-11

Love in action is the response James is seeking from his readers, but if you can limit their focus we can yet salvage their souls for Our Father Below.

By the way, I nearly forgot to mention 'keeping oneself unspotted from the world'. This forgetfulness is exactly what you need to cause by making your subjects skip over that part of the verse. What James intends is to keep his people involved in the world without becoming caught up in worldly ways. This is another avenue for us, my demon Nephew. We can immerse the vermin so deeply into the world in the name of 'service' that they become ensnared in temptation and sin. This is a case for using the Enemy's Handbook against them. Point out the passage of Paul wherein he says, "I become all things to all men that I might, by all means, save some." (*1 Corinthians* 9:22). This verse alone has allowed many of the worthless wormfood to fall into our clutches. Use it wisely and they will become so spotted by the world as to be unrecognizable as ones called out of the world by that One Whose Name we do not speak. Do your work well, Wantsome, and they'll find they're most unworthy.

> "There are many ways to describe the creatures who attempt to call themselves by the Enemy's name. Some of the ones

Memo Nine

you should attempt to brand them with are as follows:

"An invaluable person." (Of no value whatsoever)

"I wouldn't waste any time in getting to know this person." (My time's too valuable.)

"I'm pleased to say he's a former member of my church." (Thank heavens he's not here anymore.)

"Nobody could do it better." (And when nobody did we were better off.)

Excerpts from a speech by
Dr. Punjabber University of Adversity

STUDY QUESTIONS FOR MEMO NINE

How does your tongue affect the credibility of your faith?

Do you find yourself prone to slander, innuendo, or making cutting remarks in a humorous fashion to avoid confrontation? How do you suppose others see you when you do these things?

What happens to 'professing' Christians according to *Matthew* 7: 15-23 (Note vs. 22)?

What is pure and undefiled religion? (Might you consider single mothers who are the victims of divorce to fall into the category of widows and orphans?)

How might you help such people in their distress?

In what ways do we become 'spotted' or 'stained' by the world? How can we avoid it?

Memo Ten
James 2:1-7

Moving on to the second chapter of James' exasperating epistle he now addresses the issue of partiality. This is one of the most subtle of sins we entice in our victims, Wantsome, and you must take great care to twist James' words to our benefit. He has written thus:

> **1** *My brethren, do not hold the faith of our Lord Jesus Christ, the Lord of glory, with partiality.*
> **2** *For if there should come into your assembly a man with gold rings, in fine apparel, and there should also come in a poor man in filthy clothes*
> **3** *and you pay attention to the one wearing the fine clothes and say to him, "You sit here in a good place," and say to the poor man, "You stand there," or, "Sit at my footstool,"*
> **4** *have you not shown partiality among yourselves, and become judges with evil thoughts?*
> **5** *Listen, my beloved brethren: Has God not chosen the poor of this world to be rich in faith and heirs of the kingdom which He has promised to those who love Him?*
> **6** *But you have dishonored the poor man. Do not the rich oppress you and drag you into the courts?*
> **7** *Do they not blaspheme that noble name by which you are called?*

Partiality reveals a sense of values inconsistent with the message of that One Whose Name we do not speak. The Enemy

The Surelock Commentary on the *Book of James*

shows no favouritism as Peter stated in *Acts* 10:34. It is unfortunate for us that James did not use the word 'prejudice' instead of 'partiality'. No follower of the Carpenter would admit to being prejudiced, and they would have dismissed this passage as not applicable to them.

We use what we have, however, and your weapons abound here my young fiend. One tactic you may use is to emphasize James' negative comments about the rich man. Turn this into discrimination against the rich and you will still achieve your purpose in tricking them into disobeying James' command by merely reversing the victim of partiality. Remind them of the Son of David's proclamation about it being 'easier for a camel to go through the eye of a needle than for a rich man to enter the kingdom of God'. (*Matthew*19:24) Why, the rich must be horrible indeed if it is that difficult for The Enemy to accept them! Good Christians should avoid such terrible people don't you agree, Wantsome?

Another avenue available to you is to limit their understanding of the application of this story to just rich and poor. If you can concentrate their thinking on that issue then they may well forget about partiality against races, nationalities, and people of different intelligence levels or talents and abilities, or even age. Again, you have led them into following the letter of the law without grasping the heart of the law.

Do try to remember your training and give me something favorable to report to Our Father Below. Remember his 10th Commandment:

> 'Thou shalt encourage and inspire envy, covetousness, prejudice and hatred. For this shall lead to a variety of sins and broken fellowship both within the church and with the Enemy.'

Memo Ten

STUDY QUESTIONS FOR MEMO TEN

What reasons can you think of, that a person might use to consider themselves more important than another person?

What's wrong with being rich? (Or is it wrong?)

What do our attitudes toward the amount of people's wealth or poverty tell us about our walk with the Lord?

What danger does Surelock reveal regarding our attitude shift?

Favouritism comes in many forms. What other ways do we tend to judge people besides riches?

What message does the church send to the poor person when it favours the rich?

What practical ways can the church show genuine love to all people without favouritism?

Memo Eleven

James 2:8-13

Well, well, dear Wantsome, it seems you have achieved some measure of success with your victims. You actually used some of my lessons and limited their thinking to the rich vs. poor aspect of James' advice. But now you must not become complacent, for the next few verses expand on the subject of partiality and go on to speak of 'Love' and 'the law'. If manipulated correctly we can turn the minds of the woeful wimps away from these commands by pointing out their gross unfairness. The text reads as follows:

> 8 *If you really fulfill the royal law according to the Scripture, "You shall love your neighbor as yourself," you do well;*
> 9 *but if you show partiality, you commit sin, and are convicted by the law as transgressors.*
> 10 *For whoever shall keep the whole law, and yet stumble in one point, he is guilty of all.*
> 11 *For He who said, "Do not commit adultery," also said, "Do not murder." Now if you do not commit adultery, but you do murder, you have become a transgressor of the law.*
> 12 *So speak and so do as those who will be judged by the law of liberty.*
> 13 *For judgment is without mercy to the one who has shown no mercy. Mercy triumphs over judgment.*

Now, Wantsome, you realize that should they connect the old 'Love your neighbour' cliché with James' teaching on partiality it will unwind whatever nets of deceit you may have woven. Your key here is to point to the harshness of the law in not allowing for degrees of sin. James has done us a favour in one sense, by pointing to the truth that the merest stumble brings about guilt equal to the grossest sin.

The creative little creatures have devised millions of laws and codes and rules and regulations and the breaking of them has almost as many degrees of punishment as there are laws. They would no sooner kill a man for jaywalking than they would fine a man for murder, but under the Enemy's rules transgression is sin, and sin is punishable by death.

You must point out the unfairness of it all, Wantsome. Surely the 'God of Love' would not classify a little cheating on income tax in the same category as kidnapping. A little white lie couldn't possibly be as bad as rape or murder. After all, you must reason, David was a 'man after God's own heart' and look at his adultery with Bathsheba and the subsequent murder of her husband Uriah. These are the arguments you must plant in their confused little skulls. This will distract them from the realization that **no one** has succeeded in keeping the law and that is why the Son of Man came.

That thorn in our flesh, Paul, tells them 'For all have sinned and fall short of the glory of God' (*Romans* 3:23) this was the reason that it became necessary for the Enemy to send a Saviour. Only by the atoning blood of the Lamb sacrificed in the pureness of love can any of humanity come before the Enemy and be accepted.

Your mission is to keep their minds on the track of fairness. A good analogy for our benefit is that of the Enemy sitting in heaven with a scale and placing good deeds on one side and bad deeds on the other. It only seems fair that so long as the good outweighs the bad then entrance into His kingdom should be assured. Encourage this line of reasoning, Wantsome, so they might reject the scribbles of James. Don't let them realize that they are no longer under the law as Paul tells them in *Galatians* 5: 18 'If you are led by the Spirit you are not under the law', and again in *Romans* 13: 8 '… he who loves another has fulfilled the law'.

Memo Eleven

The law has always been our ally because it consistently pointed out the sins of humanity. When the Carpenter performed that dreadful self-sacrifice, He fulfilled the law for all who believe.

Mercy has indeed triumphed over judgment. The believer need only recognize (1) that he is a lawbreaker; (2) that only love can fulfill the law; and (3) only the Son of the Enemy can supply that love. Your job, Wantsome, is to confuse these truths. Convince them that the 'law of liberty' means total freedom to do anything because mercy will triumph. You know the recipe. A little truth, a little lie and mix thoroughly so the two become inseparable.

> 'All hail the power of Lucifer, let Truth not stand so tall,
> Bring forth sincere deception and crown Lies lord of the Fall
> Yes, bring forth sincere deception and crown Lies lord of the Fall.'
>
> Tempter's Hymnal

STUDY QUESTIONS FOR MEMO ELEVEN

Why do you suppose James calls partiality a sin?

Did Jesus show partiality? What verses support your answer?

Why does James call it the 'royal law'?

When James refers to the whole law, what does he mean?

The more laws there are, the easier it is to break one. God started with 10 and Jesus summed up those with just two. Why does man have such a hard time keeping them?

What is your response to Surelock's claim that the punishment is too harsh and should be based on degrees of transgression rather than such a hard and fast absolute?

Is God fair?

Memo Twelve
James 2:14-26

Well, For Beelzebub's sake, Wantsome, you must muster all the powers that you so feebly command to try and stop your subjects from pursuing any further study. Should it continue, it will lead them straight into the heart of James' message and an understanding of the relationship between faith and works. If you should fail to detract them from this basic truth then you may very well lose them for all eternity.

James knows all too well that the relationship between faith and works is the key to Christianity. What you must do is emphasize one over the other. Works without faith or faith without works, either one will serve our purpose. But before I explain let us look at the perilous passage:

> **14** *What does it profit, my brethren, if someone says he has faith but does not have works? That faith cannot save him, can it?*
> **15** *If a brother or sister is naked and destitute of daily food,*
> **16** *and one of you says to them, 'Depart in peace, be warmed and filled,' but you do not give them the things which are needed for the body, what does it profit?*
> **17** *Thus also faith by itself, if it does not have works is dead*
> **18** *But someone will say, 'You have faith, and I have works.' Show me your faith without your works, and I will show you my faith by my works.*
> **19** *You believe that there is one God. You do well. The demons also believe – and tremble!*

20 *But do you want to know, O foolish man, that faith without works is dead?*
21 *Was not Abraham our father justified by works when he offered Isaac his son on the altar?*
22 *Do you see that faith was working together with his works, and by works faith was made perfect*
23 *And the Scripture was fulfilled which says, 'Abraham believed God, and it was imputed to him for righteousness.' And he was called the friend of God*
24 *You see then that by works a man is justified, and not by faith only.*
25 *Likewise, was not Rahab the harlot also justified by works when she received the messengers and sent them out another way?*
26 *For as the body without the spirit is dead, so faith without works is dead also.*

Someday, Wantsome, we are going to find out where James gets his information. Demons believe and tremble, indeed! Who's going to believe that James has such intimate knowledge of us? The fact that it is true is beside the point. His credibility should be attacked for such a statement! On the subject of credibility try to keep your charges from looking up the *Old Testament* stories of Abraham and Rahab. On the surface, they sound like terrible people, a would-be murderer, and a harlot? These kinds of people get their works justified? What kind of God is this? Of course, it was obedience in action which proved their faith that justified Abraham, Rahab, and hosts of others throughout history. It is the same 'doers of the word' philosophy that James spouted in his first chapter.

'Faith' according to the human vermin, is defined in the verbal form as 'believe', 'have confidence', 'trust', or 'obey'. It is central to the Christian lifestyle and is one of its basic tenants. 'The just shall live by faith' is scattered throughout the

Memo Twelve

Enemy's handbook. (*Habakkuk* 2:4, *Romans* 1:17, *Hebrews* 10:38, and *Galatians* 3:11).

James insists that faith and works are inseparable. You, dear Tempter, must dilute this message. The basic laziness inherent in so many of the little dustballs should make this task easy for you. Convince them that church attendance, tithing, and Scripture reading (not studying) are works enough. This will put them into the same category as many of the Pharisees whom the Son of Mary called 'whitewashed sepulchers'.

If they are persistent in their attitude of performing 'works' then try and confine these tasks to within the structure wherein they meet on Sundays. Our fellow fiends have been excelling at this throughout the nation they call America. The subjects there have been so caught up in works within the church that the rest of the country has slipped through their fingers and is now firmly within our grasp if we take care not to push them so hard that they respond with another of their 'revival' periods.

Of course, there is always the strategy of confusing them with contradiction. For once we can use that peevish Paul's words in our favour. In *Ephesians* 2:8-9 he said 'For by grace you have been saved through faith, and that not of yourselves; it is the gift of God, not of works, lest anyone should boast'. Of course, you must stop them from continuing on to verse 10 which says that they are 'created for good works'. This is the point we confused Martin Luther on and are still somewhat successful with today. James addressed it by saying that mere mental acknowledgment was not enough, and then went on with that despicable statement about us 'believing and trembling' but you can turn that to your advantage as well, Wantsome.

Works can be used for our benefit in a variety of ways. First, you might encourage them to wait for a 'call' or until they 'feel led' to perform. What a spiritual-sounding excuse for procrastination! On the other extreme, you could get them so deeply involved in their 'ministry' that they forget who they are really working for and what the rules are. The bombing of abortion clinics was an excellent result of this tactic,

The Surelock Commentary on the *Book of James*

Wantsome. You may wish to consult with Brickdust on his strategic manoeuvres to get some ideas along these lines.

Actually, it's quite simple. If you can keep them from balancing their zeal for the work with their love for the Enemy, they will always make a mistake to one extreme or the other. They are such unbalanced boobs you hardly need do anything but distract them from calling on the Carpenter for advice. They get so caught up in 'attacking the evil' that they forget that we are their true enemy and that the people they so ruthlessly go after are supposed to be the ones that they win over in love.

If they insist on doing everything in love, then you merely turn them into passive, inoffensive creatures who won't confront, discipline, or take any aggressive action for fear of being 'unloving'. The One Whose Name we do not speak constantly confronted those who were in error about truth.

But we keep pushing Him as 'gentle, meek and mild' and His followers have bought our spiel to the point where their works are indeed worthless and their faith is feeble.

Press on, Wantsome! The battle is going our way but the war is not over yet!

> 'The amount of works your subjects will produce is in direct proportion to their spiritual maturity. So long as they are restricted to that infant stage, they are easy prey for our slings and arrows. Should they learn how to put on the full armour of the Enemy and become practiced at the arts of using their shield of faith and their sword of the Spirit, the difficulty of your task will multiply a hundredfold. You must get them committed to hiding behind their faith so that their sword rusts from disuse, or slashing indiscriminately with it so that they take it up with both hands and drop their shield. Either tactic will suit our purpose.'
>
> Professor Bucklehorn
> Battle Maneuvers 101

Memo Twelve

STUDY QUESTIONS FOR MEMO TWELVE

This section of James is the key to the entire book. In your own words, state James' main theme.

In the Middle Ages, the Catholic Church condoned 'buying indulgences', that is, paying for sins committed with good works or donations to the church. This practice was one of those which led Martin Luther to protest, saying that man is saved by faith alone, according to *Romans*. What would you say to someone who thought they could get to heaven by their works alone?

If we are to take James' words to heart, then our faith must go beyond church attendance. *Philippians* 2:12 says to 'work out your salvation'. Read that entire chapter and then consider what works you need to show your faith.

Have you ever used the excuse 'I don't feel called or led to do that'? What are some of the real reasons we shrink from work?

What do we need to do when a task presents itself?

Are we to do everything we are asked by the church? How can we discern what we should and should not do?

Professor Bucklehorn gives an apt description of two types that are all too prevalent in the church. Those too caught up in works, and those who hide behind their faith. How are we to strike a balance between these two extremes so that we can be effective warriors for God's kingdom?

Memo Thirteen
James 3:1

As James moves into his third chapter he gives us an excellent opportunity for deception. Listen to this, Wantsome:

> 1 *My brethren, let not many of you become teachers, knowing that we shall receive a stricter judgment.*

What a marvelous opening! You must certainly encourage this line of reasoning my demon friend. While a preponderance of teachers can be useful to us by multiplying opportunities for error and creating divisions of interpretation, the fewer teachers spreading the Truth the better. What James is advocating here is that teaching is a gift, in fact, one of the leadership gifts, according to *Ephesians* 4. Such gifts can be used most effectively only by those to whom they are bestowed. Fortunately, many of the moronic mudpies think that as soon as they hear something, then they are qualified to teach it. They also take great pride in their tiny knowledge and are vain enough to crave the respect a true teacher deserves. Little do they realize what error they perpetuate or how their lack of credibility turns others away from the Enemy. The writer of *Hebrews* helps us here as well, for he says they 'ought to be teachers' without qualifying any conditions.

These, however, are tactics to contradict James' teaching. What is simpler for us is to merely capitalize on a literal interpretation. All of them are called to be teachers to some extent. One cannot make disciples without teaching them something. Parents are called to instruct their offspring in the ways of the Enemy. Husbands are to be the 'priests' of their families and this would involve instructing their wives. Older brethren are to instruct new believers and older women are told to teach the younger. If we emphasize James' admonition that few are to become teachers then all these aspects will fall by the wayside and there will be less truth being spread for us to have to combat.

Use these verses to your advantage, Wantsome. Convince your subjects to turn down requests for them to teach Sunday School or lead Study Groups. James has given them a ready-made excuse for laziness, you must merely manipulate them into using it incorrectly.

You might also throw the fear of the Enemy into them as well. That statement about 'stricter judgment' could be extremely frightening to some of them. There are so many references throughout the Enemy's Handbook to the 'fear of the Lord' that we have many of them running scared thinking that the Enemy is a monstrous ogre just waiting for the little vermin to make a mistake. We've actually reversed the role of the Enemy and Our Father Below, for it is Satan who pounces on their mistakes so as to make accusations against them.

Why does the Enemy inflict stricter judgment on teachers? The people who teach should be rewarded for their efforts on behalf of the kingdom. This is the argument you must use against them. Hide their eyes from *Luke* 12:48 where the Son of David tells them 'For everyone to whom much is given, from him much will be required; and to whom much has been committed, of him they will ask the more'. A higher standard will be required of those who teach for they are representing the Enemy. This is why it is so important that only those with 'God-given' abilities pass on the teachings. For only in that way will the true message be put forth.

You must also help them to fail to realize that the judgment they face will not be entirely of the Enemy. The rest of their fellow humans will hold them to higher accountability as well. We demonstrated this most effectively in the downfall of certain television evangelists, some of whom will claim that though they have been judged harshly by men they feel they will be vindicated before the Enemy. This leads us to our next subject, Wantsome, but for now let me leave you with this parting thought:

Memo Thirteen

'Humankind fall into many categories regarding their level of commitment. Some reject the Enemy with great enthusiasm; others merely aren't looking and thus have failed to find Him. Some discover Him but fail to go beyond profession into progression of faith. All of these types are relatively easy to deal with due to their lack of understanding and ambition.

Others will attempt to combine their faith with works in a properly balanced fashion and use the gifts the Enemy has bestowed upon them according to their abilities and the level of their spiritual maturity. These will be the most dangerous, my fellow fiends. It is our duty to corrupt them into exceeding their limits of ability.

Convince them to promote themselves higher and higher, until they reach their level of incompetence. The results will not only bring them crashing down but will serve as an excellent testimony against them and their religion. They teach by their actions, my demons. Let us make sure their actions get **our** message across, rather than the Truth.'

*Beelzebub in a commencement
address at Tempters College*

STUDY QUESTIONS FOR MEMO THIRTEEN

What motivates a person to become a teacher? What **should** motivate them?

How is a teacher in the church to be different from the average member?

What dangers and attitudes must a teacher watch out for? (Note *Matthew* 7:15-23 & *Romans* 1:21-22)

Why will God judge a teacher more strictly?

What different types of teachers are there and who is called to fulfill these roles?

How can you determine if you have the 'gift' of teaching?

Memo Fourteen
James 3:2-12

How these inept little creatures come up with such excruciating pearls of wisdom is beyond comprehension, Wantsome. James must have been in direct communication with that One Whose Name we do not speak when he wrote this next section of his letter, for I cannot accept any of them having sufficient intelligence to discover these facts on their own.

It reads thus:

> 2 *For we all stumble in many things. If anyone does not stumble in word, he is a perfect man, able also to bridle the whole body.*
> 3 *Indeed, we put bits in horses' mouths that they may obey us, and we turn their whole body.*
> 4 *Look also at ships: Although they are so large and are driven by fierce winds, they are turned by a very small rudder wherever the pilot desires.*
> 5 *Even so the tongue is a little member and boasts great things. See how great a forest a little fire kindles!*
> 6 *And the tongue is a fire, a world of iniquity. The tongue is so set among our members that it defiles the whole body, and sets on fire the course of nature; and it is set on fire by hell.*
> 7 *For every kind of beast and bird, of reptile and creature of the sea, is tamed and has been tamed by mankind*
> 8 *But no man can tame the tongue. It is an unruly evil, full of deadly poison.*

> **9** With it we bless Our God and Father, and with it we curse men, who have been made in the similitude of God
> **10** Out of the same mouth proceed blessing and cursing. My brethren, these things ought not to be so.
> **11** Does a spring send forth fresh water and bitter from the same opening?
> **12** Can a fig tree, my brethren, bear olives, or a grapevine bear figs? Thus no spring can yield both salt water and fresh.

This passage, my young demon, must be twisted so as to lead your charges away from its central truth which is that only the Enemy can control the tongues of men for good and that they must continually seek Him for assistance in this area.

There are three basic attacks for your consideration as you attempt to thwart their study. The first of these is **misdirection**. Of course, this is a basic tactic for all situations wherein the little morons come close to the Enemy or His teachings. In this portion of James' writings, he has provided us with a built-in distraction in verse seven. It would be very difficult to prove that, even in this day and age, every kind of creature of the sea, as well as beasts, birds, and reptiles have been tamed. Certainly, they have their zoos and circuses and marine parks but **every** kind? This topic of discussion could keep them quite busy. See if you can't get them talking about 'killer bees' or some other rare species. (Of course, you must not allow them to look back at the verse and see that it says nothing about taming insects.)

Your second tactic is **guilt**. In verse two James says that the one who does not stumble in word is perfect. The Carpenter, according to that traitor Matthew, commanded His followers:

> 'Therefore you shall be perfect, just as your Father in Heaven is perfect.'
> *(Matthew 5:48)*

Memo Fourteen

Since none of the protoplasmic pea-brains ever come close to controlling their tongues you can instill all sorts of guilt trips on them. Remind them of some sharp reply they made or gossip they passed along. You might even bring them to the point where they decide to keep silent at times when the Enemy would prefer them to speak out. If you can convince them that silence is less offensive and therefore more 'loving' it would be a tremendous step backward in their development. We have achieved great success for Our Father Below by promoting silence by the church as a whole over the past few decades. When they should have been speaking out against abortion, immorality, removal of prayer from public schools, and dozens of other anti-Christian movements, they 'minded their own business' and allowed us to gain a tremendous foothold in the world. Now that they have found their tongues again, it is important that we encourage the opposite extreme of 'book burning religious radicals' who are completely intolerant to 'enlightened' thinking. This confuses the vermin and allows us to offer a more socially acceptable alternative in the 'New Age' movement which will one day be the only acceptable form of religion. However, that is a different topic best saved for another day.

To continue with your strategy lesson, your third option would be to instill **Hopelessness** within them. In verse eight James comes right out and states that 'no man can tame the tongue'. How delightful, Wantsome!

They are told to be perfect; then told a perfect man tames the tongue; and finally confronted with the fact that no man can tame the tongue. Ergo no one can achieve the perfection that they are commanded to strive for. So, what's the use?

The danger my young Deceiver, is that you must make them see this as an impossible command. Should they realize that it is merely a lesson to point out their need for the Enemy's help they will learn of His great willingness to instruct and assist them. At times such as those, you will find yourself denied access to their minds due to the interference generated by the Enemy's spirit within them. A direct frontal attack would be most unwise at such times, Wantsome, especially where two or more are gathered in agreement. Satisfy yourself with the fact that, if you do your job well, such entreaties by the humans to the Enemy shall be few and far between. This allows you plenty of time for counterattacks.

Our forces have made great strides in corrupting men's speech, Wantsome. The movie industry has proven especially useful for us in this regard. While the world was shocked when Rhett Butler said 'damn' to Scarlet O'Hara in *Gone With The Wind*, that word is now considered acceptable even during prime-time television. Other words that used to be considered offensive are now being pushed on young generations as the standard by which 'real' people talk. (As if Hollywood had any concept of reality!) It is especially satisfying to note the denigration of the names of both the Enemy and the Carpenter. You should find this most useful in your work, my young fiend, so remember the Third Commandment of Our Father Below as you fight for control of their tongues:

> 'Thou shalt defile the name of the Enemy so as to make it meaningless. Human tongues are to be made to utter it without regard. Their speech must not reflect any acknowledgment nor acceptance of His reality.'

Memo Fourteen

STUDY QUESTIONS FOR MEMO FOURTEEN

What formerly unacceptable words have you noticed being pushed upon society by the entertainment industry?

Does it bother you to hear 'God' and 'Jesus Christ' being used in an irreverent manner?

Why do people use 'curse' words?

What does it do to the credibility of a person's testimony when you hear them use inappropriate language? Why?

What standard are we to uphold?

How does one tame the tongue?

How should we interact with others whose speech is not pure?

Memo Fifteen
James 3:13-18

Rumours have reached me, Wantsome, of a remark you made concerning the true rank of Our Father Below. The old argument that Lucifer was created at the same time as all of the other angels and should thus be considered a brother rather than our father has brought many a tempter down into the torture chambers of Hell for 'corrective instruction'. Lucifer held a higher rank than all those who descended with him and shall thus be considered not only a leader but a true father image. I will discount this rumour as slander against you for now. But do not think your social status will protect you. On the contrary, if I should ever have proof of such infractions, I will personally see to your swift condemnation so as to spare retribution on your family and comrades for your personal deviated thinking. What I would like to see is a report from you on what you are doing regarding the next passage that your charges are studying. As I recall it reads thus:

> **13** *Who is wise and understanding among you? Let him show by good conduct that his works are done in the meekness of wisdom.*
> **14** *But if you have bitter envy and self-seeking in your hearts, do not boast and lie against the truth.*
> **15** *This wisdom does not descend from above, but is earthly, sensual, demonic.*
> **16** *For where envy and self-seeking exist, confusion and every evil thing will be there.*
> **17** *But the wisdom that is from above is first pure then peaceable, gentle, willing to yield, full of mercy and good fruits, without partiality, and without hypocrisy.*
> **18** *And the fruit of righteousness is sown in peace by those who make peace.*

The Surelock Commentary on the *Book of James*

James has identified four categories of wisdom, Wantsome, and only one of them is of any consequence to us. If you can encourage the other three in precedence over that 'wisdom from above', then you have an excellent opportunity for their corruption.

It is most fortunate that humans equate intelligence with wisdom. This makes your task more convenient to carry out. See if you can arrange to have 'intelligent' businessmen elected to positions of authority within the church. Their success in the world should make them popular among their church peers and they could easily be thrust into positions of spiritual leadership for which they are completely unqualified from the Enemy's viewpoint. This earthly wisdom for knowing how the worldly systems work is the best kind for you to promote for it has the appearance of being 'good'.

Sensual wisdom relates to the natural flesh and all the boring bipeds have this to some extent. It is really more of an instinct to meet their carnal desires. Flirtatious women are very good with this type of wisdom. They have learned how to manipulate men to achieve their purposes without actually stooping to the point of prostituting themselves. It is a very fine line, Wantsome, and they feel proud for having not crossed it. You should not be disappointed in this failure to fall into physical sin, however. We are actually better off because they feel that there has been no sin committed since no physical desecration took place. These women will arrive in our domain before those harlots who recognize their sins of the flesh and repent.

Of course, demonic wisdom needs no explanation to you. However, you must hide the source of the knowledge you impose on them lest they recognize you and call upon the Name of that One Whose Name we are forbidden to utter. This type of wisdom is best saved for those who vehemently reject the Enemy's Handbook and I wouldn't waste my time using it on your current patients.

Instead, you might concentrate on concealing true works of wisdom from above. Convince your charges that wisdom is recognized by great acts or significant decisions. This will allow

Memo Fifteen

many to go unrecognized for their small deeds of 'good conduct ... done in meekness'. Confuse them regarding the characteristics James discusses in verse seventeen. Many times we have been able to convince them that certain courses of action were 'wise' without conforming to these characteristics and it has brought them much trouble, as well as defamation to the Name they claim for themselves.

You might also corrupt their thoughts regarding 'envy' and 'self-seeking'. Should they become convinced that their efforts are 'for the Lord', then it will justify their actions in their minds. Keep them from indulging in a deep self-examination of their true motives. Surface impressions will suffice for our purposes, Wantsome.

Tradition is an excellent weapon along these lines. Just because something was 'good enough for our forefathers' or was 'always done this way before' makes them think it need never change. Truth is the only constant in the Universe my young Tempter, but if you can convince them that their way is 'wise' because of past experience without regard for conveying the Truth under current circumstances then you will have achieved a significant victory.

As to that final thought about fruit of righteousness, if you do your job well they will make no note of it. Your outline for them is thus:

Wisdom means ideas.

Ideas occur due to the perceived necessity for change.

Change sparks controversy with the status quo.

Controversy brings about opposing factions.

Factions lead to dissension and disharmony.

Disharmony nullifies peace.

Of course, again, you must keep them from those statements about 'the wisdom from above is ... willing to yield, ... without partiality ... ' etc. If they recognize a lack of peace then they will realize that the source of their 'wisdom' is not from above. This

The Surelock Commentary on the *Book of James*

works to our advantage if you can keep the opponents of heavenly wisdom stirred up. I recall a church split where the elders proceeded in true spiritual wisdom but were opposed by deacons attempting to maintain the status quo. The elders had sown their seed of wisdom in peace and all who supported them maintained a peaceful attitude and eventually were proved correct because their fruit was righteous. The faction that supported the deacons provided us with a most delightful display of envy, self-seeking, backstabbing, name-calling, and hypocrisy. Of course, some were sincere but had they recognized the characteristics of the wisdom from above exhibited by the elders and sought the will of the Enemy instead of their own, we would not have enjoyed the delightful spectacle of those debates and gossip and the 'democratic vote' so essential to the American mind. I leave you with these final thoughts, my young demon.

> Wisdom, without humility is what we must promote.
> Or better yet, let them determine wisdom by majority vote!
> Let them claim superior wisdom as grounds to criticize,
> Feuding over meaningless trifles, thinking themselves so wise.
> Keep them distracted, my fellow fiends, from reading the Enemy's Book.
> This will keep them from finding true wisdom, and someday we'll watch them cook.
>
> Maltknife
> Poet Laureate Underworld Subsector 6

STUDY QUESTIONS FOR MEMO FIFTEEN

How do we recognize true wisdom?

What are some of the motives behind those who promote their own 'wisdom'?

Is the majority always right?

If the majority seems to be against you, how do you react?

Does wisdom always result in great deeds or decisions? Give some examples.

How can one gain wisdom from above?

Memo Sixteen

James 4:1-3

As James begins his fourth chapter he addresses somewhat, the subject I ended my last memo with. That is, the lack of peace when improper wisdom is implemented. I trust you have learned from your cousin Wormwood's failure of 1941 (by their calendar) that war is of little consequence to us and, in fact, can be most disastrous to our cause by turning more of the clay clods toward the Enemy for help and comfort.

Now let us go over the text again before I continue.

> **1** *Where do wars and fights come from among you? Do they not come from your desires for pleasure that war in your members?*
> **2** *You lust and do not have. You murder and covet and cannot obtain. You fight and war. Yet you do not have because you do not ask.*
> **3** *You ask and do not receive, because you ask amiss, that you may spend it on your pleasures.*

What James is alluding to here is the conflict between prayer and pride. Naturally, your task is to build up their pride so that they fail to pray. Of course, you must do so subtly. One of our best weapons is that old cliché 'The Enemy helps those who help themselves', which sounds very scriptural and therefore seems appropriate to the task at hand. You must keep them from discovering that this statement is nowhere to be found in the Enemy's Handbook.

If they should happen to turn to that menacing manual, you are to distract their thinking toward the activities of the historical characters. Have them look to see the things that were **done** rather than the things that were **said** prior to the deed. Great battles and buildings, and acts of courage can be excellent sources of inspiration. Use them to your advantage, Wantsome. Encourage dissatisfaction with current conditions and press them to do something about it 'for the Lord'. So long as they fail to actually ask Him what to do. Their human logic is so pitiful that you can easily lead them down the primrose path of their own selfishness.

If you can convince them that they are fighting for what they 'deserve' and that the ends justify the means, so much the better. If they should get around to 'asking' then you must stop them from heeding James' warning about asking amiss. Turn their prayer into a one-way monologue rather than a conversation. There are dangers inherent in allowing them to pray, but if you are cautious, prayer becomes an excellent tool for us.

For if in their prayer they 'ask amiss' then it is highly likely that the Enemy will not grant their request and they will become acutely disappointed and faltering in their faith. On the other hand, if they should succeed by their own power and force of will then their selfish prayer will be seen as magical and they will continue in a false faith pouring out their requests like wishes to a genie.

This may even be a case where you can point them to another scripture (very carefully, however) and corrupt the Carpenter's own words. In *Matthew 7:7-8* they are told to 'ask, seek and knock' and promised that they will 'receive, find and have the door opened'. This seeming reinforcement of their false conception will do even more damage when their plans go awry because they will think they had a scriptural foundation for their prayer.

However, Wantsome, I cannot emphasize enough the danger in allowing prayer at all. Should they learn how to do it correctly you may lose them forever. If the Enemy or one of His angels interferes, you will be powerless and subjected to their bidding. I need not remind you of what happened to Legion.

Memo Sixteen

If they gather together to ask for His blessings, we hasten to implant their selfish desire.
We keep on oppressing until it gets depressing
And they march out on their own, through the muck and the mire
Beside them to guide them in covetous lusting; Ordaining, maintaining their pride at all cost
So from the beginning, their minds we keep on spinning, until, when all is done, their battle is lost.

Tempter's Hymnal

The Surelock Commentary on the *Book of James*

STUDY QUESTIONS FOR MEMO SIXTEEN

What is the source of quarrels and conflicts?

Why would Christians ever have quarrels and conflicts?

What motives really cause our conflicts?

How do we 'justify' our causes?

What may be missing from our prayer life if we're not getting answers?

Why does the Bible condemn envy and covetousness?

Where do the things we truly need come from?

How can you use that fact to adjust your attitude?

Memo Seventeen
James 4:4-10

I cannot emphasize enough how imperative it is that you should disrupt your subjects' study of these next few passages, Wantsome. James not only advises the vermin on doing away with pride and becoming humble before the Enemy, he also gives them a powerful strategy for dealing with us in particular. A strategy so simple, yet so profound, that it forces us to depart from them for invaluable periods of time while they often find their spiritual strength being reinforced. These periods of banishment can easily tip the battle in their favour, Wantsome. That is why you must never allow the little bags of blood and bone to discern your presence, at least not at your present rank and training, for you would be no match for the powers that would be brought against you.

Read the upcoming portion for yourself and you will realize its inherent danger.

> 4 *Adulterers and adulteresses! Do you not know that friendship with the world is enmity with God? Whoever therefore wants to be a friend of the world makes himself an enemy of God*
> 5 *Or do you think that the Scripture says in vain, 'The Spirit who dwells in us yearns jealously'?*
> 6 *But He gives more grace. Therefore He says: 'God resists the proud, but gives grace to the Humble.'*
> 7 *Therefore submit to God. Resist the devil and he will flee from you.*
> 8 *Draw near to God and He will draw near to you. Cleanse your hands, you sinners; and purify your hearts, you doubleminded*

The Surelock Commentary on the *Book of James*

> **9** *Lament and mourn and weep! Let your laughter be turned to mourning and your joy to gloom.*
> **10** *Humble yourselves in the sight of the Lord, and He will lift you up.*

To your advantage, James immediately insults his readers by referring to their adultery. Of course, this will register to their microbrains as the sexual lust of forbidden human relationships and, if they have not so transgressed, will incense and prejudice them toward James' advice. Naturally, what he is actually referring to is that the Enemy calls the church to be the Bride of the Carpenter. When they turn away, as they often do, to the temptations of this world, they reject their true husband. Of course, you can turn this scripture to your advantage by so compounding their guilt feelings as to have them withdraw completely from worldly entanglements. If they are not serving their community, witnessing to their neighbours, voting in their elections, and helping the less fortunate in the Son of David's name; then they are nearly worthless because their faith lacks works. It is a lovely paradox, Wantsome.

If the pride we've discussed in my past few memos is found to be insufficient then you can try switching your tactics to make them yearn for humility. Just be sure you make them aware of their great humility so that they take pride in the fact of it. False modesty has always been one of our greatest instruments for destruction. You could even use the Enemy's Handbook against them. This time let them turn to Matthew's infamous book and read these passages:

> *Therefore whoever humbles himself as this little child is the greatest in the kingdom of heaven.*
> *Matthew* 18:4

> *And whoever exalts himself will be humbled, and he who humbles himself will be exalted.*
> *Matthew* 23:12

Memo Seventeen

The harder you make them work for humility the more pride they will take in their 'accomplishment' and when the rewards seem insignificant or lacking you will have an excellent breeding ground for discontentment and contempt.

Should they, however, submit to the Enemy, He will call attention to your presence and you will be in grave danger. Our Devilish Defense Department has yet to come up with anything that can protect us from submission to the One Whose Name we do not speak. Should they raise their shield of faith in protection and wield the sword of the Word against you, His mighty power will hurtle you to unimaginable depths.

Unfortunately, James has listed criteria to help them become submissive. Your best strategy here is to convince them of the absolute ludicrousness of taking James literally and therefore rejecting him altogether.

How does one 'draw near to God'? Since the Enemy is in heaven perhaps your subject should go climb a mountain. Of course, 'cleansing one's hands' most thoroughly will be a tremendous help too so they had better take some disinfectant soap along. Purifying the heart must have to do with diet. Better watch that cholesterol! Lamenting, mourning and weeping ought to do wonders as well. Laughter turned to mourning and joy turned to gloom will really make a good impression at the office. What a wonderful witness for the faith! Now if they can just figure out where the Enemy is looking, they can be sure to perform their acts of humility at just the right place and time ...

Of course, Wantsome, we know that these acts refer to examination of the outward lifestyle, purification of motive, acknowledgment, and repentance of sins, etc. This would bring your subject into an all-out state of war against you. That is why you must be extremely careful. If they ever see themselves for what they really are, they will realize that they are powerless before the Almighty Enemy and yet have all His power at their command against us. This is why pride is so important, my demon fiend. It is Our Father Below's greatest accomplishment and is responsible for where we are today.

The Surelock Commentary on the *Book of James*

Time to cause trouble my fiends, trouble
  on earth in every city
With a capital 'T' and that rhymes with 'P'
  and that stands for pride
Got to cause trouble,
  yes, trouble indeed my fiends.
Gotta keep on filling mankind with pride
  until they're fried!

from The Music Fiend

STUDY QUESTIONS FOR MEMO SEVENTEEN

How does one 'draw near to God'?

What is 'friendship with the world'?

What does it mean to be in the world, but not of the world?

Why does James call us to 'lament, mourn and weep'?

How do we cleanse our hands and purify our hearts?

Describe how you might 'resist the devil'?

What power makes the devil flee from you?
(Note the warning in *Acts* 19: 13-16)

How do you practice humility without becoming proud of it?

Memo Eighteen
James 4:11-12

John Calvin, one of the infamous instigators of the Protestant Movement, once wrote of his species, 'Hypocrisy is always presumptuous and we are by nature hypocrites, fondly exalting ourselves by calumniating others'.

I realize you occasionally have trouble with their language so I will inform you that 'calumniate' means 'slander'. Thus, we find that humankind is aware of its tendency to judge others and speak evil even though hypocritically. James addresses this topic as well in the next passage of his book.

> **11** *Do not speak evil of one another, brethren. He who speaks evil of a brother and judges his brother, speaks evil of the law and judges the law. But if you judge the law, you are not a doer of the law but a judge.*
> **12** *There is one Lawgiver, who is able to save and to destroy. Who are you to judge another?*

We always encourage humankind to think of themselves in the image of the Enemy, just as it says in *Genesis*. For by doing so the rabble always credit themselves with too much power and wisdom. They dare to think of themselves as little gods, or pieces of one giant god and therefore assume powers and authority that are, in reality, beyond their comprehension.

Instead of sharing the love of the Enemy or going out and telling others the Good News, we must keep encouraging them to look to the *Old Testament* judgments as examples of how they should go about the Enemy's business. You must keep them from adopting a 'Love the sinner, hate the sin' attitude. (Although that too can be manipulated to our favour.) Keep them on the attack and convince them that their intentions are good. After all, they are only trying to help the other person to understand the error of his ways. If they do not judge, how can they be expected to distinguish from good and evil?

If you fill their minds with these types of thoughts, perhaps they will justify their actions to themselves. Little will they realize that if they fail to heed James' advice, they will be ignoring one of the Carpenter's commands, for He told them 'Judge not, that you be not judged. For with what judgment you judge, you will be judged ...' (*Matthew* 7:1-2)

One tactic you may wish to employ is that of Sympathetic Reciprocal Judgment (SRJ). You should recall this from your basic course in the human ego, but I will reiterate it for you. This is that justification with which we tempt them to 'point out the speck in their brother's eye' so long as they are willing to allow examination of their own 'eye'. This of course would promote growth and a cleansing of sin within the brotherhood as a whole. The flaw in their thinking, which you must hide from them, is that humans very rarely see 'eye to eye' when it comes to criticism. The SRJ tactic can generally be manoeuvred to result in name-calling, an increase in defensiveness, a fallout of fellowship, and an overall loss of love within the brotherhood. This, of course, creates prime conditions for an influx of all sorts of temptations on your part. As I recall Archdemon Ringrock actually convinced some of the parasites that they possessed the 'gift' of criticism. What a marvelous coup for him. It was certainly a prime factor in his promotion.

Keep this in mind, Wantsome. You might even allow them to read *Ephesians* 4:15 where Paul tells them to 'speak the truth in love'. So long as you exaggerate the action while deviating the motive, you have an excellent chance for success.

> 'Humankind has a tremendous capacity for destruction in their efforts of construction. In personal relationships they tear one another down in their attempt to build themselves up, resulting in the breaking of the Carpenter's 2nd commandment.

Memo Eighteen

You, my students, must capitalize on that tendency. You must fill them so full of thoughts of their own progress that they become blinded to the disaster that surrounds them. Use those weapons of pride and ego to make them appear righteous unto themselves.

They are such weak-minded creatures that they can easily be manipulated into justifying their actions. They can truly be misled into believing that 'in His image' is equivalent to being a part of Him that has authority to judge others.

Keep them off-balance in this regard and when they complete their building of themselves they will find their work burned up by their own judgments upon arrival in the fires of Hell.'

Archdemon Ringrock
Tempters Conference #1611

STUDY QUESTIONS FOR MEMO EIGHTEEN

In this context what does it mean to 'judge'?

If one does not judge, how do we distinguish good from evil?

What is the difference between this type of judging and that found in *Matthew* 7:15-20?

Since James says, 'Do not speak against one another, *brethren...*' does this mean we can speak against, and judge those who are *not* Christians? Defend your answer with scripture.

Why is it dangerous to judge one another?

Rather than judge each other, what should our relationship be towards each other?

Memo Nineteen
James 4:13-17

No doubt, Wantsome, you have heard of the unfortunate circumstances surrounding Tempter 1st Class Vancat. In spite of his rank and training, he allowed himself to push a patient too far and found himself overpowered by Enemy forces. His being cast out will, of course, meet with a severe reprimand and appropriate punishment from Our Father Below. I only mention it due to the fact that he was overseer of a group similar to yours, only a little more mature in their faith. Let it serve as a warning against overextending your power my fiendish fellow, for you have never actually faced the Enemy head on and I assure you it would be most unpleasant in both the short and long term.

Back to the matter at hand, James is now addressing the topic of planning for the future. If you have been following standard procedure, your subjects will be sending their prayers up as requests for the Enemy to grant, or plans for which they seek a 'rubber stamp' approval. Should this passage inspire a change in their prayer habits your best weapon is to encourage the waiting game. But I've gotten ahead of myself. Let us look at the passage before I continue.

> **13** *Come now, you who say, 'Today or tomorrow we will go to such and such a city, spend a year there, buy and sell, and make a profit';*
> **14** *whereas you do not know what will happen tomorrow. For what is your life? It is even a vapour that appears for a little time and then vanishes away.*
> **15** *Instead you ought to say, 'If the Lord wills, we shall live and do this or that.'*

> **16** But now you boast in your arrogance. All such boasting is evil.
> **17** Therefore, to him who knows to do good and does not do it, to him it is sin.

Now, where was I? Oh yes, the waiting game. While I touched on the tactic briefly in Memo Twelve let me reiterate it for you. James has here attacked the sin of presumption, which is a display of pride, our favourite weapon. By manipulating the thoughts of your subjects, you could carry them to the opposite extreme, wherein they make no plans because they are waiting for the Enemy to show them what to do. Since so many of them are inept at communication with Him, they can generally be made hesitant over ideas that come to them by questioning, 'Is this from (the Enemy), the devil, or me?' While they are wrestling over the question they can be made to miss many opportunities for service and blessing. The paralysis of analysis is one of my favourite strategies when used properly.

At particularly discouraging times you might use that statement about life being a 'vapour' to pass along thoughts of suicide. But you must be extremely careful here, Wantsome, this is exactly where Vancat failed. In fact, at your present level of training, I must insist that you limit yourself to whispering passing thoughts in this area. Perhaps after this assignment, should you succeed, you can arrange continuing education courses at the University of Adversity to properly prepare you for such advanced temptations.

Another factor you will have to watch for regarding your subjects' search for His will is their study of the Enemy Handbook in an effort to understand how His principles work. In this area, you can lead them into all sorts of inappropriate behaviour. The misuse of 'casting lots' or 'putting out fleeces' can bring about catastrophic results in their lives, but if they learn how the Enemy works through a thorough study of scripture then they become much more effective at fitting into His plans. You must also endeavour to discourage them from investigating all their options and discussing the situation with others who have some spiritual maturity. If you can keep their

Memo Nineteen

blinders on and focus their attention in a limited direction then they could very well miss opportunities that would provide solutions to their dilemmas. But if you allow them to overcome their pride and share their situations with others for the purpose of seeking advice then they might actually multiply what tiny power their brains have and discover enough wisdom to find the Enemy's will.

Fortunately, we have taken most of them through enough experiences of ridicule when they shared a private matter that they are usually reluctant to risk the gossip and betrayal that could befall them. You, my young minion, must help them to stand firm in their belief that they don't need anyone else but the Carpenter. Keep them away from those miserable *Proverbs* about 'seeking wise counsel', or other scriptures that encourage gathering together or building up one another. If they should become convinced that they need to seek out another opinion, try to lead them to a poor choice of confidants. Don't let them ask the Enemy who they should talk to but encourage them to plunge ahead assuming that one Christian is as good as another since they are all believers. This will lead to grave errors and should provide you with many opportunities for discouragement and disenchantment with the Christian life as a whole.

That final verse about 'knowing to do good and not doing it' leading to sin, of course, refers to the sin of omission. I trust you remember your training in this area. Instill your subjects with a fear of confrontation and rejection. Convince them of the irreparable damage that would be done to their social position or career status. Use their families and friends to dissuade them from 'inconvenient' courses of action. Anything you can throw at them to give them an excuse for not doing the Enemy's will is acceptable. Involve them in discussions about the difference between His perfect will and His permissive will, if you can handle it. Just remember to keep them talking and not acting. It is their actions that count, Wantsome. The works that prove their faith is your primary target for obliteration.

The Surelock Commentary on the *Book of James*

'Just a closer walk with sin, that's your goal my young fiends. Help men follow all their whims and lean on their own pitiful understanding and their sin nature will usually do the rest for you. As long as you disrupt all communication with the Enemy you should be able to keep them following their own destructive path.'

Miscommunication
A Fiend's Best Friend
By Dr. Scalebucket

Memo Nineteen

STUDY QUESTIONS FOR MEMO NINETEEN

What advice does James give about making future plans?

When you make long-range plans but short-term steps start to go wrong, what do you do?

How have you seen the Lord use circumstances to show you His will?

What does it mean to you, 'you are just a vapour'?

Why is it considered arrogant to boast about our plans?

What does verse 17 mean to you?

Have you ever felt led by God in one direction, but instead did something else that you wanted to do? What happened?

What steps will you take in the future to discipline yourself into following God's plans?

Memo Twenty
James 5:1-6

Now we enter into that final chapter of James' drivel wherein he addresses a variety of subjects. In fact, his propensity for changing subjects can work to your advantage, Wantsome. If you can overload your victims with outside activities so that they are tempted to take on larger portions of scripture for study in an effort to finish more quickly, then they can be more easily manipulated to gloss over verses in a hasty manner and miss some of the pearls of wisdom that a more detailed study would reveal.

James begins this chapter with yet another address on the subject of riches.

> 1 *Come now, you rich, weep and howl for your miseries that are coming upon you!*
> 2 *Your riches are corrupted, and your garments are motheaten.*
> 3 *Your gold and silver are corroded, and their corrosion will be a witness against you and will eat your flesh like fire. You have heaped up treasure in the last days.*
> 4 *Indeed, the wages of the labourers who have mowed your fields, which you kept back by fraud, cry out; and the cries of the reapers have reached the ears of the Lord of Sabaoth.*
> 5 *You have lived on the earth in pleasure and luxury; you have fattened your hearts as in a day of slaughter.*
> 6 *You have condemned, you have murdered the just; he does not resist you.*

In this particular passage, James appears to be condemning the rich and you can certainly use that to your advantage,

The Surelock Commentary on the *Book of James*

Wantsome. He seems to imply that all riches are sordid gain. If any of your subjects are rich, they must have gotten that way through evil means and you can use that impression against them. It might provide an ideal way to split up that study group you are overseeing. If you can build up a prejudice against the wealthier members over such passages as these and then stir in envy and covetousness, justified by a concern over spirituality of course, then you can hope for one of two scenarios to occur.

First of all, there could be a haughtiness and an attitude of justification for their condition which could put them on the defensive. If you manoeuvre it properly you may even create an air of superiority within them so that they look down on their accusers as 'lower class'.

Secondly, they may take these comments to heart, even if they are not true in their particular circumstances, and take steps to change their lifestyle. Should this occur and they begin to give up their riches in exchange for performing service for the Enemy, then you will have an opportunity to assail them with problems that their riches could have easily allowed them to avoid and make them long for their wealth and upper-class lifestyle again. Such disillusionment can be most useful as you can imagine.

The truth is, that riches can be gained by honest, hardworking means, and people of integrity, can maintain a wealthy standard of living without resorting to lying, cheating, or unfair business practices. Since such people are rare, however, you can usually lump them into a typical stereotype that fits the mould James has outlined. Naturally, the Enemy can use the rich for His purposes as well as anyone. If a Christian gains the respect of wealthy businessmen by showing how to be a wealthy businessman with Christian principles, then he can be a valuable asset to the Carpenter's work. As one of the little vermin has said 'Someone's got to witness to the millionaires in Beverly Hills'.

The warning that James is giving is that they must be careful about how they gain and how they use their wealth. The Enemy sees all their actions and their motives. Your mission is

Memo Twenty

to help them justify their activities in their minds and deny any thoughts of greed or avarice by creative excuses. The more you help them fool themselves, the more they'll think they are justified before the Enemy and the better our position in the battle for their souls.

For your convenience, I am including several successful excuses developed by the Devilish Department of Intelligence (DDI) in the past.

(1) The ends justify the means. (One of the classics)

(2) Cheating on taxes is permissible since:
- The government wastes so much of our money.
- I don't agree with government policies.
- I can do more good with it than they can.
- Our tax system is unfair anyway.

(3) Underpaying employees is permissible because:
- They're stealing from me anyway.
- I never get a full day's work from them.
- That's the standard of the industry.
- They get other benefits, like company discounts.
- They'd just blow it on drinking or drugs.

(4) I need to save for my retirement.

(5) I have to have luxury cars, a ski boat, a mountain cabin, etc. in order to maintain the image of my position and impress my clients, and associates.

(6) The more I have, the greater my tithe to the church. (One of my personal favourites)

(7) I've never hurt anyone. I've only taken from the rich (insurance companies, banks, etc.) who overcharged and misled people to get it in the first place.

(8) (The Enemy) helps those who help themselves.

The Surelock Commentary on the *Book of James*

I'm sure you'll recall others as you review your training manual. Keep me informed of your progress.

STUDY QUESTIONS FOR MEMO TWENTY

What do the terms 'moth-eaten garments' and 'gold and silver are corroded' mean to you in light of this passage?

Why is the term 'heaped up treasure in the last days' significant?

Do you ever have ambivalent feelings towards people you know whom you consider wealthy? Have you examined your reasons for feeling that way?

Why does James tell the rich to 'weep and howl'? What miseries do you suppose are coming upon them?

Have you ever found yourself using any of the excuses Surelock lists for justifying greed?

Read and discuss *Proverbs* 3:32, and *Proverbs* 15:8.

Memo Twenty-One
James 5:7-11

Patience is a virtue, my dear Wantsome, greatly to be admired in other people. This is the next subject that this pitiable preacher pontificates upon. So long as you can get your subjects to admire patience in others and not practice it themselves you can nullify what James is attempting to teach at this point in his letter.

The passage now goes on in this manner:

> *7 Therefore be patient brethren, until the coming of the Lord. See how the farmer waits for the precious fruit of the earth, waiting patiently for it until it receives the early and the latter rain.*
> *8 You also be patient. Establish your hearts, for the coming of the Lord is at hand.*
> *9 Do not grumble against one another, brethren, lest you be condemned. Behold, the Judge is standing at the door!*
> *10 My brethren, take the prophets, who have spoken in the name of the Lord, as an example of suffering and patience.*
> *11 Indeed we count them blessed who endure. You have heard of the perseverance of Job and seen the purpose of the Lord, that the Lord is very compassionate and merciful.*

James now appears to be addressing those who are the victims of the rich people he just condemned in the previous verses. I addressed the subject of endurance in my second memo to you regarding this *Book of James*, and you may recall I specifically warned you against allowing the vermin to cross-reference the *Book of Job*. Here we find James encouraging them to remember Job's patience and those of the prophets as well.

You must again distract them from looking back to the *Old Testament* stories. Keep their minds satisfied with taking this verse at face value, for that is damaging enough.

The analogy of the farmer can be easily twisted to your advantage, Wantsome. You either convince them that, like the farmer, they must continually work the fields to help the crop grow and then push them into overworking the conditions toward their objective so their goal or 'crop' becomes a failure; or you assure them they should do nothing while waiting for their 'crop' and while they sit back you send in the crows of adversity and the weeds of despair.

Verse eight can be useful to you as well. What does it mean 'Establish your hearts'? You could lead them on a merry chase with that one. Are they to maintain good health? Should they seek love and marriage? What James is teaching is they need to adopt an attitude that is loving, trusting, and accepting of the Enemy no matter what trials and tribulations may come their way. Rather than become angry or discouraged they are to maintain a peace within for they will not be forsaken. But if you keep their eyes off the Son of David and on their circumstances you should prove successful.

The second half of that verse is most promising. Since it is now some two millennia after its writing, you must seriously press the question 'Where is this Son of Man? Why hasn't He come back? What's He waiting for?' Because the weeping wimps are so tied to time and the Enemy has a timetable that's operating on an eternal schedule, it is very easy to frustrate them. They forget the centuries that Israel was enslaved in Egypt and the generations that suffered captivity by various nations. Certainly, this is the longest period of His removal from Israel's presence since that nation began, but then, what more fitting punishment could there be for their rejection of their messiah?

The cults we've instituted have been most helpful in this aspect among the gentiles. They keep predicting His return and keep missing the mark. It merely continues the prejudice and ridicule of the world against all of Christendom as incompetent

Memo Twenty-One

fools. Our mastery of the media has been most excellent in these cases.

Of course, they may take the view that their life is but a grain of sand on an eternal beach, in which case it doesn't matter if the 'coming of the Lord' is the second advent or merely His coming in spirit to take them into His kingdom at the end of their earthly existence. In either case, their patience would be rewarded. It would, of course, be best if you discourage this dangerous attitude, Wantsome, or at least twist it to such an extreme that your subjects lose all interest in their purpose for living.

James calls those who endure 'blessed' and the Son of Mary, in that agonizing address on the mountainside referred to endurance when He said,

> 'Blessed are you when they revile and persecute you, and say all kinds of evil against you falsely for My sake. Rejoice and be exceedingly glad, for great is your reward in heaven, for so they persecuted the prophets who were before you.'
>
> *Matthew* 5:11-12

Your best tactic to combat this teaching is to keep your subjects busy. Either keep their minds so occupied that they have no time to think of heavenly rewards, or create such a fixation on heavenly rewards in their minds that they fail to take the necessary actions to obtain them. (Remember, 'Faith without works is worthless!').

I sign off with a selection of inspiration from Our Father Below.

> 'My fellow fiends, fountains of the forces of evil that you are, I feel that it is necessary to remind you, once again, of certain factors regarding human failing. The foolish fodder, whilst in their present state, are limited by the concepts of time

The Surelock Commentary on the *Book of James*

and space. Whereas space forces them into a physical condition where we are able to exhibit our fiendish influence through the method of materialism, time is often a much-neglected weapon.

Time is on our side, my demon warriors. We have the ability to help them waste it on unprofitable pursuits; to overcrowd their schedules so as to bring about frustration, fatigue and even physical malfunction; to position them into periods of perilous despair that tries their patience; and bring about a general worry as to how to handle a future over which they have almost no control, but think they have much.

I want a new manual of strategies, tactics, and battle manoeuvres drawn up for our trainees immediately that will cover this topic. I want no more defeats due to endurance!'

Excerpt from a memo to the **DDI**

STUDY QUESTIONS FOR MEMO TWENTY-ONE

Define patience.

What does it mean to 'establish your heart'? How does one do that?

Look back to the stories of Noah, Moses, and Elijah. Note how many years each had to endure suffering and be patient.

What lessons do we learn from the story of Job?

What does the analogy of the farmer tell us? What are some of the mistakes we could make as we look toward our 'produce'?

Who is the Lord full of compassion and merciful toward? Do you fit in? What does that mean to you and how does it affect your attitudes and actions?

Memo Twenty-Two
James 5:12

As I informed you previously, James' tendency for rapid changes of subject can be well worked in your favour. After starting this chapter with an address to the rich regarding the misuse of wealth, he suddenly decides to give a teaching on patience. Now he has elected to comment on the subject of swearing, but only for one verse, for he will change topics again in verse thirteen.

Naturally, you can easily confuse your victims into skipping right past this single verse. If they should be organized enough to find it then you can certainly convince them of its minimal importance since James' treatment of it is so brief.

James is practically quoting the Carpenter when he states:

> **12** *But above all, my brethren, do not swear, neither by heaven nor by earth nor with any other oath. But let your 'Yes' be 'Yes,' and your 'No,' 'No,' lest you fall into judgment.*

As you will note, this swearing is not taking the Enemy's name in vain, which would be an obvious repetition of one of His commandments. Rather, it is regarding verbal statements of fact or contract. The Carpenter's remarks can be found in *Matthew* 5:33-37 and He reveals even more than James by attributing swearing to Our Father Below.

Throughout the centuries, however, we have infiltrated mankind's laws and lifestyle to the point where swearing beyond 'Yes and No' is common practice and does not necessarily have the meaning it did in James' time.

That is precisely why it is still so useful to us. Because James' warning seems outdated it is not taken seriously anymore. This allows us to continue the evil that takes place under this practice with no one the wiser.

One of their 'scholars' has expressed the idea that the 'judgment' referred to might be construed to mean both heavenly and worldly judgment. He contends that, if a man's intent was evil, he would suffer the consequences of the Enemy's judgment; whereas, no matter what his intent, if he were to swear to a contract that failed to come to pass, his worldly possessions would be diluted due to the legal judgments imposed by human courts. It is an interesting hypothesis and is true to some extent, but your main concern is to distract and confuse. If this hypothesis helps you to muddle their thinking, use it as you see fit.

The legal system and the business world have done much to help our cause in this regard, Wantsome. They have made it virtually impossible for anyone to get by with merely a 'yes' or a 'no' and you must point this out to your charges to provide an example of how obsolete the Enemy's Handbook has become.

James has put up a warning sign and you must blind them to it. Take them off on tangents, lead their discussions astray. Do your duty, my demonic disciple!

> There is a statement I love to hear, when men
>   assign something worth.
>
> It sounds like music in my ear,
>   when they swear and take oaths on the earth.
>
> Oh, how I love swearing,
>   the oaths and contracts their sharing.
>
> The promises that they are bearing
>   when broken will make them all ours!
>
> Tempter's Hymnal

Memo Twenty-Two

STUDY QUESTIONS FOR MEMO TWENTY-TWO

Why do you suppose James addresses the topic of swearing an oath or contract in this context?

Why is his address so brief?

Solomon also addresses the subject of contracts. Read *Proverbs* 6:1-5. What makes oaths and contracts dangerous?

Jesus gives us more insight into swearing starting in *Matthew* 5:33. Read this passage and note that it comes right after his comments about divorce.

Have you had experience with someone who made a promise and failed to keep it? What was your reaction? What does that tell you about Christians making promises while the world watches?

How much control do you have over your life and circumstances? What should that tell you about swearing with an oath?

How can you relate this teaching from James to your current lifestyle?

Memo Twenty-Three
James 5:13-18

I must advise you, Wantsome, that I am not at all satisfied with the lack of progress you are showing with your subjects. You have failed to convince any of them to drop out of the group and their disagreements over interpretation have been trifling and insufficient to lead to any major confrontation. You have stirred up no dissension among them at all.

Need I remind you that the mere circumstances of their meetings can be used against them? Uncomfortable conditions, lack of preparation, mixed up time schedules, and even problems over refreshments can stir up trouble! Do I have to think of everything for you? I remind you once again that this assignment will figure prominently in your next promotion review and I will not tolerate substandard performance.

Now, this next section of James will supply you with several avenues of opportunity. Pay attention and you may yet accomplish your mission.

> 13 *Is anyone among you suffering? Let him pray. Is anyone cheerful? Let him sing psalms.*
> 14 *Is anyone among you sick? Let him call for the elders of the church, and let them pray over him, anointing him with oil in the name of the Lord.*
> 15 *And the prayer of faith will save the sick, and the Lord will raise him up. And if he has committed sins, he will be forgiven.*
> 16 *Confess your trespasses to one another, and pray for one another, that you may be healed. The effective, fervent prayer of a righteous man avails much.*
> 17 *Elijah was a man with a nature like ours, and he prayed earnestly that it would not rain; and it did not rain on the land for three years and six months.*

18 *And he prayed again, and the heaven gave rain and the earth produced its fruit.*

Most of your fellow demons have been so successful at counterattacking these conditions I would assume that it would be unnecessary for me to instruct you, however, since your record is not favourable let us continue.

First of all, James addresses suffering and his advice is to pray. That pontificating Paul of Tarsus wrote to the Thessalonians 'Pray without ceasing' (*1 Thessalonians* 5:17) and indeed, if the mental midgets were to maintain such a posture, we would be hard-pressed to corrupt them. As you are aware, there are many techniques to disrupt or deaden their prayers. I will elucidate a few but I suggest you review your Training Manual.

If you can't distract them from going to their knees then you must turn their thoughts toward trivial matters. The question 'why?' is always a useful distraction. It worked very well, for a time, with Job and his wife and friends. What the creatures fail to realize is that 'why?' is usually not important. The fact that they live in a fallen world is usually reason enough for their difficulties.

Try to keep them from asking 'what?'. If they should start petitioning the Enemy with 'What do you want me to learn', or 'What do you want me to do for You?', then you will run into trouble. Whenever you allow a two-way conversation and give them the opportunity to listen, your subject is in danger of being lost.

Other types of prayer you must inhibit are the cry for help, when accompanied by an understanding of the reality of who they are and their true relationship to the Enemy; also the prayers of thanksgiving and praise. If the driveling deposits of DNA remember that they are to 'give thanks always for all things' (*Ephesians* 5:20) then you will find any suffering you cause them to be nearly useless.

James next advises the cheerful to sing psalms. My advice is to let the cheerful rejoice in celebration all you want. The greater the party the better. But don't allow the thought of

Memo Twenty-Three

singing psalms, or acknowledging the Enemy's part in their cheerfulness, to enter their heads. Remember, your strategy is to have them blame the Enemy when things go wrong ('Acts of God', 'Why me Lord?' etc.) and credit themselves when things go well.

All this talk about healing of the sick has raised much uproar throughout the history of the church. We have been able to convince certain sects that medicine is anathema and many a victim has fallen due to people trying to be 'faithful' to James' teaching. It is clear from this and other passages of the Enemy's Handbook that healing is possible through men who are gifted by the Enemy to do so. But James also mentions the anointing of the sick with oil. What you must keep your readers from discovering is that oil, in James' time, was used as medicine. The proper analogy of James' scenario is that both medicine and prayer are to be applied to the sick for their healing and then trust the results to the Enemy's will.

The comment about 'if he has committed sins, he will be forgiven' is another trap you must be ready to spring. In order for a prayer of faith to be genuine enough to save the sick, it must include repentance for sins that may have led to the sickness. James has not stated that sickness is caused by sin, but that is what you will implant in their minds and the minds of their friends. It was a most effective technique with Job's friends and is still quite useful to us today.

It is most fortuitous that the pride instilled in them from the time of Adam and Eve is a natural deterrent to verse sixteen. They are not likely to confess their trespasses to one another except under the most conducive of circumstances. I suspect that even you can manage to deny them such conditions. Create the doubt in their minds that they have no need of healing and the need for confession disappears. Of course, they all need healing for they are all 'sick' with their sin nature and they all have something they could confess, but among Protestants you will find it rare and among Catholics you will find its meaning so convoluted as to render it nearly harmless to your endeavour.

The Surelock Commentary on the *Book of James*

Finally, those verses about Elijah should be dismissed as an old fairy tale, illogical and totally exaggerated. I trust that you can take it from here. Remember old Feverwart's words:

> 'Into the battle I verily go, seeking recruits from the Enemy. Onward I plod seeking revenge, for my Father's defeat at Calvary.
>
> By lies and by pain I lead them astray ne'er revealing my true identity.
>
> Through deceit and cruel jest I play with their minds 'til their 'faith' is a mass complexity.
>
> By hook or by crook, through truth mixed with lie it's a matter of great dexterity.
>
> But someday I shall stand with my Father Below and receive my reward for eternity.'

STUDY QUESTIONS FOR MEMO TWENTY-THREE

What kinds of suffering do we go through? List some examples.

How would prayer have helped in the examples you just listed?

Often men blame God when things go wrong and take the credit when things go well. How **should** we react to good times?

What is your reaction to situations where prayer does not result in healing? How would you apply verse 15 in those times?

While it may be argued that all sickness is the result of sin's entrance into the world at the Fall, are all sicknesses that you and your loved ones experience the result of specific sins in your lives? Why is the answer important? (See the *Book of Job*)

What are the roles of doctors and medicine in treating sickness? (Note: *John* 9:1-7)

Why is it difficult to 'Confess your trespasses to one another'?

What dangers are there in confession?

How often do you pray for someone other than yourself? How will you improve that ratio?

Try the **CATS** method in your prayer time:

> **C**onfession of your sins.
>
> **A**doration of your Lord.
>
> **T**hankfulness for His loving kindness.
>
> **S**upplication for the desires of your heart, entreatment for others, and His will to be done.

Memo Twenty-Four
James 5:19-20

In his closing passage, James now switches from the subject of physical healing to that of spiritual healing. We have been able to use these verses as the spark for great argument and debate resulting in church splits and even denominational divisions. Those great church factions of Calvinists and Arminians keep going back and forth over whether or not this passage denies the doctrine of eternal security and have provided Our Father Below with much amusement.

So long as you encourage ideological debate at the expense of practical application you should meet with satisfactory results. Let us look at this final word from James' poisonous pen:

> **19** *Brethren, if anyone among you should wander from the truth, and someone turns him back,*
> **20** *let him know that he who turns a sinner from the error of his way will save a soul from death and cover a multitude of sins.*

Aside from the obvious distraction of doctrinal debate, there are other tactics you may put to use for those subjects who actually attempt to employ this teaching.

First, you may wish to confuse them with the idea that only the Enemy can truly convert someone, and that if it is within His will then it will be done, so why should they be the ones to risk the rejection? This will usually lead them into the old predestination debates and again distract them from their true purpose. We know that the Enemy has **foreknowledge** of all who will come to Him as individuals, but He does not **predestine** any single person, for this would be a violation of free will. That is why we continue to attack everyone in our path, they are all up for grabs.

The fickle frames of flesh fail to understand that the Enemy predestines a 'class' of humankind, so it were. He has predestined that this class or group will be the ones He allows to enter into His kingdom. He then gives all the creepy creatures the opportunity to enter that class through their acknowledgment and acceptance of that One Whose Name we do not speak as their Lord and Saviour. If they meet the criteria of the class, they meet the criteria of those predestined and are saved.

But most of them don't know that. They go on with their debates and differing doctrines and that is to our delight. As I have said before, Wantsome, if you can keep them talking, they won't be listening to Him or acting on His commands. This will be most conducive to your goal.

Another ideological proposal to implant regards that final statement about covering a multitude of sins. Tell your subjects that it is the sins of the one who saves the backslider that will be covered. This will confuse them into thinking that humans can atone for their own sins through works, and since works have been a main emphasis of James, this should fit into their minds quite easily, even though erroneous.

In truth, it will be the sins of the one saved from the error of his ways that will be covered by the blood of the Lamb. The important truth, which you must hide in a maze of philosophical hedging, is that anyone who has turned from the truth is in danger and needs to be brought back through invitation, prayer and love. In many cases, Wantsome, the one who has strayed and returned truly becomes a new creature with pure motives and becomes a most inconvenient witness against us. I caution you with all earnestness to blockade such an occurrence.

> Redeemed! What an awful condition.
>
> Redeemed by the blood of the Lamb.
>
> Redeemed how my heart burns to say it,
>
> Another soul lost to 'I Am'

Memo Twenty-Four

Redeemed, redeemed,

No food for Our Father Below.

Redeemed, redeemed,

The fires of hell will not glow.

Wailing Song
Tempters Hymnal

The Surelock Commentary on the *Book of James*

STUDY QUESTIONS FOR MEMO TWENTY-FOUR

What are some ways you have observed 'Christians' straying from the truth?

What should we do when we observe someone in that situation? (Note: *Matthew* 18:15)

This passage has sparked much controversy over the issue of eternal security. But no matter which side you take, there is a more practical issue at stake here. What is it, and why is it more important than the theological debate?

What would you say to someone who thinks they are saving their souls from death and covering their multitude of sins by claiming this passage as they go witnessing door-to-door, or pass out tracts on the street corner?

Who really saves souls and what are some of the ways it's done?

What is your role in saving souls?

Epilogue

Well, my dear Wantsome, I've given you my best strategies regarding the manipulation of the *Book of James* in the Enemy's Handbook. What can I expect from you in return? Your progress has been most unsatisfactory. Not a single soul have you been able to report as ready for our consumption. You have been given the best training within my power, often at the neglect of my other duties. While you have not yet failed to the point of losing anyone completely as your cousin Wormwood did in 1941, you are dangerously close to demotion. I ... Wait, who are you? What are you doing? This is outrageous! I am the Under-secretary of ... aaagh!

(At this point the dictation stops, a scuffling sound is heard and the recording begins again in a new voice.)

Wantsome! Special Agent Flysprocket here. We've just taken Under-secretary Surelock into custody. I thought I would send this recording along as my personal congratulations on your efforts to expose the old demon's heresies. Your reports and the evidence you supplied showing him actually saying that 'Name we do not speak' were most instrumental. Even though he was quoting the Enemy Handbook, Lord Lucifer's orders in this matter are quite clear. Our Father Below will be most appreciative of your patriotism I'm sure. Wouldn't be a bit surprised if you didn't find yourself with a new position at Infernal Civil Service. Maybe eventually Surelock's job, eh? Well thanks for all your help, mate. The old boy's getting a bit testy so we'd best get him off to headquarters. Long live the Prince of Darkness!

Appendix

THE TEN COMMANDMENTS OF LUCIFER

1. Thou shalt misdirect the priorities of humankind so that their energies focus on worldly things, ideas or people ~ to the point where these become their 'gods' instead of the Enemy.
2. Thou shalt instigate the creation of religious symbols and talismans toward the object of idol worship.
3. Thou shalt defile the name of the Enemy so as to make it meaningless. Human tongues are to be made to utter it without regard. Their speech must not reflect any acknowledgment nor acceptance of His reality.
4. Remember to deplete the true meaning of all holidays.
5. Thou shalt instill selfishness and disrespect toward older generations.
6. Thou shalt encourage the justification of killing and 'survival of the fittest' attitudes.
7. Thou shalt implant all manner of deviant and indecent sexual desires.
8. Thou shalt promote stealing and the justification thereof.
9. Thou shalt always mix truth and lies to confuse humankind and shall encourage them to do likewise to each other.
10. Thou shalt encourage and inspire envy, covetousness, prejudice and hatred. For this shall lead to a variety of sins and broken fellowship, both within the church and with the Enemy.

A FINAL WORD TO THE BIBLE STUDY GROUP

He has delivered us from the power of darkness
and conveyed us into the kingdom of the Son of His love,
in whom we have redemption through His blood,
the forgiveness of sins.

Colossians 1:13-14

www.ingramcontent.com/pod-product-compliance
Lightning Source LLC
Chambersburg PA
CBHW061951070426
42450CB00007BA/1206